MORE MONEY
NEW MONEY
BIG MONEY

Creative Strategies for Funding Today's Church

Wayne C. Barrett

DISCIPLESHIP RESOURCES
MATERIALS FOR GROWTH IN CHRISTIAN FAITH AND LIFE
P.O. Box 189 • Nashville, TN 37202 • Phone (615) 340-7284

Library of Congress Card Catalog No. 92-76039

ISBN 0-88177-120-1

DR120

CONTENTS

FOREWORD

The task of financing the church today can seem absolutely over-whelming. *Changing demographics, changing economies, and changing membership or attendance patterns can make the fund-raiser's task a moving target. Yet certain fundamentals exist that are appropriate components for any fund-raiser's artistry. This book attempts to highlight some fundamental issues that can improve, even revitalize, fund-raising in the church.*

This book focuses on three general themes: More Money – strate-gies for improving existing performance; New Money – strategies for attracting income from heretofore untapped sources; and Big Money – strategies for major gift development. Hopefully local church lead-ers will find this functional division helpful in identifying tasks most appropriate for their own particular situations.

Much of what is presented here has been learned from over a thousand onsite consultations with local congregations. Over these past eleven years I have encountered just about everything that can be found in a local church setting, and each experience has been instructive. This synthesis of frontline gleanings is presented with the hope that the reader will avoid many of the pitfalls I encountered. It can be tough out there, but I remain convinced that the best days of finance in the church are yet to be. My prayer is that you may find this resource a true catalyst for your work as a leader in the exciting congregations of today and tomorrow.

Part 1

MORE
MONEY

1 | CREATING THE CLIMATE FOR COMMITMENT

A congregation I know seldom receives pledges in excess of 50 percent of its budget and must rely on unpledged giving and fund-raising campaigns to cover the costs of ministry. Yet, simultaneously, another congregation routinely subscribes 90-105 percent of its budget every year. What's the difference?

After years of observing this phenomenon, I am convinced that the difference is nothing less than the fruits of radically different *climates* for the practice of stewardship. The members of the first congregation give less, not because they have less to give, but because the climate for giving in their local church tends to inhibit rather than enhance their personal stewardship. However, I am convinced that such a situation can be changed and a healthier environment created. In some situations a congregation can achieve this transformation in as little as a few months, whereas other congregations may require several years for the climate to improve. Although consultation from afar is always somewhat presumptuous, I offer the strategies below in the context of "what *I* would do."

START WITH THE PASTOR

Whether or not the problem was caused by the pastor, the solution must begin there. A poor climate for commitment is frequently a spiritual problem, a leadership problem, and an administrative problem. The pastor is crucial to each of these issues. If the problem is spiritual, the pastor may be the catalyst to address the matter. Whether by preaching, counseling, or witnessing, the pastor sets the spiritual tone for a committed style of spirituality within the congregation.

Often the problem of poor commitment climate is a lack of leadership. Here as well, the pastor may be the key player. Leadership is largely about vision and the pastor must have a vision of where the congregation is to go. Is pledging to be encouraged here? Who will start the process if not the pastor?

We frequently run into clergy who declare, "Money is not my 'thing'." I'm always amazed. Not their "thing"? Would they say the same about preaching or prayer or the sacraments? Of course not. Yet the number of persons whose commitment deficiency is due to a lack of preaching or sacraments is small indeed compared to those who experience no leaders to follow into a life of authentic discipleship. We will address later the roles of the clergy and laity in the stewardship life of the church. For now, however, let us observe that the pastor's leadership is often the only catalyst capable of moving a church toward commitment.

IT'S A MATTER OF STYLE

The commitment atmosphere in a church is often the product of "styles." A church that emphasizes individuality over cooperation will have a difficult time encouraging commitment. If my values are most important, why be concerned about anyone else? Why indeed?

Basic to this issue is the style of the church's image or marketing plan. Today it is common for churches to emphasize numerical growth and to scramble for new members through advertising and other marketing strategies. I applaud those congregations that have succeeded in attracting new members, but beware — the very image that brought them in may stand in the way of stewardship growth.

An old story tells about a couple experiencing marital problems. As is so common in a marital crisis, there was a complete communication breakdown, and the couple agreed to go see the pastor. But they did not respond to the pastor's counsel. The pastor tried all the tricks of the counselor's trade but had no success. Finally, out of frustration or insight, the pastor got up from behind her desk and walked around to where the couple were seated. Not knowing what to say, the pastor simply bent down and gave the wife a great big hug. The wife began to smile and fairly glowed with joy. Obviously she had not had a good hug in a long while. Triumphantly, the pastor turned to the husband and declared, "Did you see that? That's the sort of thing she needs more of! What are you prepared to do about it?"

The man thought for a moment and then replied honestly, "Well, I could bring her in on Tuesdays and Thursdays for some more."

I submit that this is a paradigm of today's church. We have become a church so consumer-oriented that we have forgotten the basic principles of the incarnate church. Not only have we been called by God to be *consumers* of the blessings of the kingdom but to be *producers* as well.

What is the style of your congregation? Is service or being served emphasized? Does the worship atmosphere resemble an audience of theatergoers or the Body of Christ? How is money discussed in your congregation — as a necessary evil or as a symbol of lives and values?

Take a hard look at the liturgy used in your local church. Are words such as *commitment, covenant, affirmation, profession of faith, pledge,* or *vow* used in the worship service? These are the words of commitment.

How is the offering viewed? Please tell me that you do *not* call the offering a "collection." Read Exodus 29 to discover something of the flavor of an "offering" rather than a mere "collection." (An excellent resource to give vitality to your congregation's liturgical life is Hilbert Berger's *Now, Concerning the Offering,* available from Discipleship Resources.) Is the offering introduced, or does it intrude on the service? Is the offering seen as a symbolic opportunity to respond to the worship experience, or is it buried in the perfunctory preparations for preaching? Is a *prayer* of consecration offered? These and other simple strategies can do much to make the offering a focal point of your congregation's life together.

EXPECT COMMITMENT

Educators have known for years that children will live up to (or down to) the level of expectations placed upon them. When little is expected, little is produced. Over a period of years, many congregations have so de-emphasized commitment that pledging is seen as a rather nice option for those who care for that sort of thing.

Break out of that mold of low expectation! Establish that commitment is *expected*. In all communications with the membership, present the idea that a pledge is basic and the minimal performance standard and that persons in this congregation are expected to make a financial commitment!

Evaluate current practices (more on this later). Do the persons in the congregation know that a financial commitment is expected? I have seen campaign literature that was so low-key no one could recognize that pledging was being described.

Do you notice when no pledge has been received? If you take no remedial action when a person fails to make a financial commitment, you are reinforcing the attitude that commitment is unimportant. At the very least, a follow-up mailing should make clear that you are aware that no pledge has been received. Even better is a follow-up phone call. The caller confirms that the local church has no record of a pledge having been made and provides several options for the prospect:

   a. Make the commitment now over the phone.
   b. Bring or send the pledge card to the church this week. (You will call again if necessary.)
   c. The caller will make an appointment to pick up the commitment card.

This is not intended to be a high pressure exercise but rather a clear statement about the importance of making a financial commitment.

Be prepared to meet objections head-on. Many persons in today's churches will look you squarely in the eye and declare, "I don't believe in pledging." This response is similar to that of the child who announces at the dinner table, "I don't like broccoli." Persons who wear their pledge-aversion on their sleeves are revealing a spiritual immaturity that requires remediation. While a parent can force the child to at least nibble the broccoli, we seldom can require pledging in the voluntary church. Instead we must deal at the level of expectations.

Listen to the reasons a person may give for refusal to pledge. Drop the word *pledge* and use a more positive word, *commitment*. Even those persons, bold in their denunciation of pledging, will not likely object to making a commitment. Yet more than semantics is involved. "Pledging" sounds contractual and legalistic. "Commitment" is the language of faith and is consistent with other elements of the faith — baptism, membership, conversion. I have never been very comfortable with the term "estimate of giving." Although *estimate* is more user-friendly than the word *pledge*, it lacks any spiritual or theological validity. An estimate is a term from the business world, and though less threatening than contractual language, it attempts to make what should be a faith statement into a transaction. Go ahead and use the word *estimate* if you must, but please don't justify it on the basis that "the church needs to know its future income." Persons need to make a financial commitment or estimate, not to give the local church fair warning, but to understand the *essential difference between stewardship and fund-raising.*

ENLARGE OWNERSHIP BASE

Persons relate to one another and to the church in different ways. When a healthy commitment climate exists within the congregation, financial matters are discussed openly just as important issues would be discussed in a family setting. A healthy church environment is like a healthy family.

Families sometimes disagree and even quarrel, but the fundamental assumptions about ownership are not in dispute. Expenses, no matter who benefits, are family expenses and the appropriate responsibility of the entire family. A healthy congregation recognizes this relationship and avoids divisions between "us" and "them."

In a congregation where persons feel a healthy sense of ownership, commitment comes naturally. When the ministry is something persons relate to and believe in, they will easily support it financially. If your local church is having financial difficulties, now may be the time for evaluation. Do the majority of your members feel a sense of ownership of the ongoing program? Or are the programs the proprietary interest of only a few leaders? Church leaders who have the advantage of plenty of information and input opportunities, can easily presume that *everybody* has the same relationship. This is seldom a valid assumption. Often the "rank-and-file" in a congregation are ignorant about financial matters until it's time to pay the bills!

It's better to discover that the family is in conflict over a proposed expenditure *before* there is a bill to pay; and mere voting may not be an adequate signal of support for a project or ministry. It's easy for a few leaders to raise their hands at a board meeting. However, if you really want financial support for the ministry, including a wider circle of persons in a meaningful sense of "ownership" will be crucial.

Thus, a major task is to work on increasing the stream of information flowing within your congregation. The best information stream is two-way. The leadership must communicate with the membership, and the membership should communicate with the leadership.

CHANGE CAN HAPPEN!

As one who has worked with over 400 local congregations over the past ten years, I have enjoyed seeing dramatic improvement in the stewardship climate in scores of congregations. Persons *can* change. Improvement *is* possible. You may be the catalyst to change the very atmosphere of commitment in your congregation.

By permission of Johnny Hart and Creators Syndicate, Inc.

2 | PLEDGING: Why It Works in Increasing the Level of Giving

When I was a boy there was a special Sunday every year when we were invited to "take the pledge." This pledge was to abstain from alcoholic beverages. It was a solemn occasion. Each year some persons signed pledge cards and forswore alcohol while many other persons simply watched.

Today that rite has been all but forgotten within our congregations. Sadly, many congregations appear to have abolished any other form of pledging as well. In many local churches there is no opportunity for persons to make a commitment at all. This is more than a sad passing of a powerful tradition. Something is wrong.

Commitment has been at the very heart of Christian discipleship since Jesus recruited Peter and Andrew ("Come, follow me . . ."). Clearly that invitation was more profound than a mere request for a contribution. It demanded their entire lives! In the 2,000 years since that first expression of commitment, one dimension continues without change: The quality of the Christian life is directly related to the person's *commitment.*

Pledging allegiance to Christ is an integral part of one's faith. Similarly, pledging a portion of one's financial resources to the cause of the kingdom is an essential part of a person's stewardship. A congregation that offers no opportunity for persons to declare their allegiance to Jesus Christ will, inevitably, suffer from a spiritual tepidity. This lukewarm faith is non-sustaining. In much the same way, a congregation that offers no opportunity for persons to commit their resources will, without much doubt, discover a lack of financial staying power.

Several years ago the Rockefeller Brothers Fund commissioned the research firm of Yanklovich, Skelly, and White to survey giving patterns of Americans. Their report, "The Charitable Behavior of Americans" (published by Independent Sector, 1828 L Street NW, Washington, DC 20036), included this dramatic finding: Persons who made a financial commitment gave significantly more than those who didn't.

Is this surprising? Of course not. What is absolutely striking, however, is how much more pledgers give. According to the Yanklovich data, regular churchgoers who made no financial pledge gave an average of $440 per year to the church. Persons who made a financial commitment expressed as a fixed dollar amount gave an average of $880 — exactly double that of non-pledgers. Furthermore, persons who pledged a percentage of their income gave even more, an average of $1,220, almost three times what the non-pledgers gave. To say that pledging makes no difference is not intellectually credible.

Since pledging plays such a demonstrable role in the giving pattern of churchgoers, let's examine several reasons for this phenomenon. By taking a look at *why* pledging influences giving, we may be better able to provide methods concerning *how* persons can do so.

1. *Pledging transforms an occasional reflex into an ongoing commitment.* Sometimes I feel like making a gift; sometimes I don't. If I allow my current feeling level to determine what I give, my giving will be sporadic and very likely will amount to a lower total contributed. A pledge will supersede my current feeling and motivate me to do what I know I should whether I feel like it today or not.

"Reflex" donors are plentiful in most local churches. These are persons who respond to a particular appeal just because they feel like it today. Perhaps you've noticed an occasion when someone who rarely makes any big gifts makes a particularly large gift to a special appeal — perhaps for camp scholarships. Suddenly this $10-per-week donor makes a $200 second-mile gift. Next year, when you ask for camp scholarship money, however, the same donor gives $10. What's going on? This is likely to be the reflex phenomenon at work. In the first instance, the donor was moved to make the larger gift. Perhaps the motivation was having a child or grandchild going to camp for the first time, receiving a recent financial windfall, or experiencing some other special circumstance. For whatever reason, the feeling was not the same the second time around.

Even when the giving is directed toward the operating budget, reflex giving is very much in evidence in many congregations. In its purest form, the Sunday offering becomes a barometer that measures the atmosphere of the congregation. When good feelings are evident, the giving increases. When conflicts or problems arise, the giving plummets. In some cases the offering becomes a financial rating system evaluating last week's (or today's) sermon. Clearly the pledge system can provide needed relief from this phenomenon.

2. *Pledging separates giving patterns from attendance patterns.* One truism of church finance is the close relationship between giving and worship attendance. This phenomenon was described in my earlier book, *The Church Finance Idea Book* (see "For Further Reading," page 153), and was given the name "Barrett's Law." Barrett's Law recognizes that giving and attendance are linked and declares, "When they park it in the pew, they plop it in the plate."

For those who attend worship every week, the incentive for giving is not a problem. But what of those whose attendance pattern is not so regular? What possible incentive is there to give for the weeks one is absent from worship? Traditional strategies have stressed loyalty. Letters have been written reminding (scolding?) sporadic attenders that the congregation's expenses go on every week. To this the absentee may reply, "So what?" Loyalty seems to be a particularly weak argument to those who, if they were loyal, would be more regular in attendance in the first place.

For a vast and growing group of members, worship attendance and giving is analogous to going to a movie. These persons would not dream of walking into a theater without paying (buying a ticket). By the same token, these persons would never consider sending money for times when they were not present. Who wants to pay for a movie not seen?

Pledging provides a basis for regular giving regardless of attendance. When a person commits $520 per year to the church, he or she is saying something quite different from "$10 every week I'm in attendance." In the first case, the commitment translates into $130 per quarter, whereas the second case may be no more than $120 annually if the attendance pattern is once per month.

3. *Pledging provides a basis for proportionate giving.* In the long run, the local church that stresses *stewardship* will experience

increased giving. Basic to this understanding is the concept of "proportionate giving" — giving a committed portion of one's financial resources.

Committing a percentage of one's resources, whatever the percentage may be, is a faithful way to practice stewardship. Giving becomes "giving what's right instead of what's left." This "first fruits" concept is not only biblical, it is a proven way to encourage growing contributions. According to the Rockefeller data mentioned above, religious givers who try to give a certain percentage of their income to a church or synagogue each year gave a mean percentage of 4.6 percent of income, whereas religious givers who did not give a percentage contributed a mean of 1.5 percent of income.

4. *Pledging provides a framework for the local church to assist the donor.* When a donor has made no commitment to the congregation, what can the local church do to encourage growth in giving? Probably not much. There is little reason to send monthly or quarterly statements, for to non-pledgers they are no more than receipts.

For pledgers, however, the church can do much to help the donor grow as a giving steward. Regular statements of contributions can inform and encourage the giving of those who have made a commitment. (See Chapter 8 on statements.)

A current pledge may be the basis upon which an increase in giving is made. Part of the difference between stewardship and fundraising is the rationale for growth in giving. As one evaluates his or her giving level for the coming year, the pledge should be based upon growth goals as a steward rather than whether or not the church happens to need more money.

5. *Pledging builds charitable giving into the financial plan.* As more and more persons are receiving financial planning assistance, philanthropy should be built into the plan as a basic expression of the donor's value system. A financial plan will look quite different when contributions are based upon "what I want to accomplish with my finances" rather than "what I'm giving now."

Pledging is consistent with the *intentionality* of financial planning. A pledge is an expression of steps toward a goal, precisely what financial planning is all about.

3 PAVLOV'S CARD CURE

I van Pavlov won the 1904 Nobel Prize for his research in conditioned reflex response. What he learned from dogs can be useful for us to remember when we work with church members. Persons (and dogs!) are creatures of habit. When we wish to change the behavior of our friends in our congregations, we would do well to ease them into the new behavior with a pattern of similar actions.

One behavior we frequently wish to encourage is the making of a financial commitment, a pledge. Yet many persons recoil in horror at the very sight of a commitment card. Signing a pledge card may be a foreign behavior, one which will require some "un-learning."

BEGIN WITH SOMETHING FRIENDLY

Rather than having a pledge card as the first card the prospect encounters, why not create a series of cards for response? Start with those that are least threatening and move sequentially toward a financial response.

Schedule a series of four or more Sundays in your commitment campaign, and ask worshipers to complete a card each week. Each week (and card) emphasizes a different aspect of the congregation's ministry.

WEEK 1. Give each worshiper a card (a blank 3" x 5" card will do). During the worship service invite the worshipers to write on the card something they really like about their local church. Collect the cards with the morning offering. Alternative themes for this first card might include: "My favorite thing at (name of church) is . . .," "What first attracted me to (name of church) is . . .," and "The greatest gift (name of church) has given me is . . ."

WEEK 2. Cards received the previous week may be displayed in the narthex of the church. (Attach ribbons to the cards and suspend them from the narthex ceiling.) Persons inevitably will wander among the cards and peruse the various responses.

Upon entering the sanctuary, worshipers receive another card. This week they are directed to reflect upon the *people* of the congregation and to list names under the heading: "Someone who has meant a lot to me in (name of church) is . . ." Persons will record names of past and present Sunday school teachers, pastors, friends, and a variety of the "saints" of the church. (This exercise may be accompanied by a soloist singing a song such as "Wind Beneath My Wings.")

However you administer the mechanics, you will be helping the congregation reclaim the personal dimension of its life together. Parishioners will appreciate this opportunity to reflect upon the truth of the Avery & Marsh song "We Are the Church" that says "The church is not a building, the church is not a steeple, . . . the church is a people" (Hymn 558 in *The United Methodist Hymnal*).

MOVE TO SOMETHING FUTURE-ORIENTED

WEEK 3. Just as last week, display the cards in the narthex. Persons arriving for worship will wander among the cards, and, once again, be flooded with memories of persons who have touched their lives. It's a powerful introduction to worship.

Now, shift the focus from the past to the future. This week the bulletin will contain a third card. The invitation today is for persons to think about the future of the congregation and to record on the card their wish or prayer for their church. This causes worshipers to think seriously about the future and to consider what their local church might be like if money were no problem. What would our church be like if it could be exactly like we *want* it to be?

For a third time we have encouraged the worshipers to ponder the meaning of the church in their lives.

WEEK 4. Once again the narthex is aflutter with the cards received last week. Persons arriving will need plenty of time and space to wander among the cards and to peruse the visions for the church of their fellow members. This whole process will trigger an atmosphere of positive, hopeful thinking.

This fourth week is Commitment Sunday. The card in the bulletin today is a pledge card. (You'll need to mention that today's cards will *not* be hung in the narthex!)

Some congregations have had good results with a special means of collecting commitment cards. Instead of receiving these in the offering plates, invite the persons to bring their cards to the front of the sanctuary and to place their commitment cards on the altar or on the communion rail. Consider having a special receptacle, such as a model of your local church or a basket containing symbols of loaves and fishes.

Having the members of the congregation bring their commitment cards to the altar or communion rail reinforces the special nature of this offering. Consider ways to build this high moment into your Commitment Sunday worship service.

Will previously pledge-adverse members really fill out a commitment card today? Will the experience of filling out three less-threatening cards reduce "card anxiety"? Not in all cases, of course. But if only one person makes his or her first financial commitment, in my judgment this makes the entire exercise worthwhile. Someone will be going beyond making a *contribution* to making a *commitment*.

Not addressed by this four-Sunday exercise is the phenomenon of persons who attend only once or twice during this period. In many churches this is a significant segment of the congregation. It is true that these folks will miss much of the reinforcement of the Card Cure. Nevertheless, experiencing even one week of this program will show that you truly do want more than dollars. You will have invited both positive and negative feedback. You will have encouraged persons to remember the personal element of the church, while reflecting upon individuals who have made the church what it is. Each of these exercises has substantial "stand alone" value by itself.

The goal of the Card Cure is to encourage persons to invest themselves in the church. Whether this investment is feedback through words or the commitment of funds, each person completing a card develops a healthy awareness that this local church is the place where God touches their lives.

4 | Broadening the Base

The most obvious solution to the problem of too few donors in a congregation is to recruit additional members. If this were all that easy, however, I'd write a book about evangelism and probably sell a lot more copies. The more likely solution in most local churches is to expand the core of committed donors within the existing membership.

If making that first financial commitment can increase the level of giving (and we have already asserted that it does), it is clearly in our interest to encourage commitment from donors who have previously not responded. To achieve this goal, special attention or targeting will be necessary.

In my earlier book, *The Church Finance Idea Book*, I examined eight common methods of soliciting financial commitments:

a. Personally written letters   *e.* Small group meeting
b. General mail appeal   *f* Telephone canvass
c. Loyalty Sunday   *g.* Personal visitation
d. Congregational dinner   *h.* Saddlebag method

Each of these methods has strengths and weaknesses. We will not take time to evaluate them now except to observe that methods A, B, and C are not oriented toward base expansion and, not surprisingly, do little to increase the number of commitments received. Similarly, methods D and E will not necessarily increase the number of commitments, unless special efforts are made to secure commitments while the persons are present at the event. Once the prospect leaves the banquet or cluster meeting, his or her enthusiasm (and likelihood of pledging) drops considerably.

This leaves three methods — telephone canvass, personal visitation, and saddlebag — that are well suited to expanding the financial base. Let's examine each method with an eye toward what works and why.

TELEPHONE SOLICITATION

If you had asked me ten years ago if the telephone would ever be a significant tool in receiving financial commitments to the local church, I would have been very skeptical. Yet, here we are in the '90s and the telephone is a very "hot" tool indeed. The telephone can be useful either as the primary commitment-gathering device or as a supplementary tool to support a Commitment Sunday or similar plan.

Phone every family that has not been heard from after Commitment Sunday. Divide the prospects carefully into two categories: 1) those likely to make a commitment (frequently donors of record but with no pledge history) and 2) those *not* likely to make a commitment.

Persons who have made few or no contributions of record this year should not be asked by telephone to pledge. Instead, ask a few carefully crafted questions to discover any needs they may have that the local church may be able to serve. Occasionally these persons respond well to "opinionnaires" or questions inviting their responses to questions about program possibilities for the congregation.

If you believe that the prospect to be phoned is a true pledge prospect, however, be certain to ask: "Have you considered what your commitment for 199__ will be?" If an affirmative reply is received then ask, "And what is the weekly amount of that commitment?"

One group that can be contacted by phone with good results is non-renewing former pledgers. Almost every congregation will have some persons who, though they made a commitment the previous year, will not renew this year. Don't let them develop bad habits! A number of congregations I have worked with report good results from the "play dumb" strategy.

Call these previous-pledgers and explain that you have not received their pledge card. Ask, then, if it will be all right if you simply renew them at last year's rate until this year's pledge card can be found or until they send in another one. Occasionally there will be a good reason why no pledge card has been turned in: The donor is upset, moving away, unemployed, or some other reality. More common, however, is the fact that the donor just has not gotten around to it. Most former pledgers will renew at this time by default, but the responsibility to take the initiative belongs to you.

THE SADDLEBAG METHOD

This generic method refers to a variety of specific incarnations — Pony Express, Circuit Rider, Iron Horse — and a plethora of variations on the same theme. In each of these methodologies the congregation is divided into geographical units called circuits, routes, or the like. Participants take the receptacle of commitment materials (saddlebag, envelope, album, or other device) to the first home on their list. The materials are left with the resident at that house who similarly moves the materials to the next house and so forth.

This method works for a variety of reasons. Without much doubt the biggest reason for its success is the fact that everyone must deal with the campaign materials. No one will be overlooked, at least in theory. Thus the Saddlebag Method can be effective for broadening the financial base of the congregation. Almost axiomatic is the fact that the more persons who are actively involved in any campaign, the more likely it is that additional persons will make commitments.

Persons who wish to explore this method a bit further may wish to obtain a copy of the Circuit Rider Commitment Program (see "For Further Reading," page 153). This low-cost manual is available through Cokesbury. It is an excellent introduction to the mechanics of any Saddlebag Method.

PERSONAL VISITATION

The most likely means for expanding the financial base of your church undoubtedly is personal visitation. That this is true can be observed by noticing the method chosen by fund-raising professionals who are evaluated on performance results. When you truly want a response you go in person.

Visitation is an excellent way to meet people where they are. Meeting people where they are makes fund-raising tremendously adaptable and keeps it completely consistent with the view that stewardship is individualistic. A personal visit can elicit a response that no mailing can produce.

Why does visitation work so well at obtaining that first commitment? Let's list a few reasons:

a. As with the Saddlebag Method, the issue of commitment must be dealt with. Although the prospect may refuse to make a commitment, the decision must be active. Many campaigns allow persons to decline by default. A visit requires a response.

b. The visitor has an opportunity to discover any impediments to commitment. Often the prospect only needs to re-establish some human contact with the church. The personal nature of the visit frequently enables this to take place.

c. Refusal to make a commitment is not only a rejection of the church and its leadership but of the person visiting. This is difficult for most persons to do.

Broadening the financial base is an absolute necessity for active congregations. Sooner or later every congregation will experience a shrinking base through natural attrition — death, relocating, and so forth. Unless intentional efforts are undertaken to expand the financial core of contributors, the financial vitality of a local church will be crippled.

Don't let more than three years go by without a commitment campaign that is intentionally oriented toward base expansion.

5 | UPGRADING THE LEVEL OF GIVING

M any congregations do not have the luxury of a growing membership to provide additional revenue, and steps may already have been taken to broaden the financial base. Thus the remaining question is, "Where do we go now for financial growth?"

The answer for most congregations in this predicament is to work at increasing the level of giving from current donors. This concept, what professional fund-raisers call "upgrading," can result in larger increases in church income than most base expansion strategies. Below are several proven strategies that can lift the level of contributions from current donors.

STRATEGY 1. GO WHERE THE MONEY IS

I have a friend who once ran unsuccessfully for governor of his state. I say "unsuccessfully" only in the sense that he failed to be elected. Although failing to gain election, he nevertheless ran a strong campaign and received the votes of thousands. "What," I once asked him, "did you learn from that political experience?"

I would not have been surprised had he pondered the question for a while. Instead, he replied immediately, "If you want to pick fruit, go where there's fruit on the trees." He went on to describe how he had spent too much valuable campaign time in precincts that were hostile to his political views. Rather than convert the hostile voter, he simply wasted time he might have used seeking to influence friendly or undecided voters.

I submit that this is a parable of church stewardship practice. How easy it is to look at the disparity in giving levels among our membership and conclude (falsely) that the place to put our efforts is among those who aren't giving. But, as my friend learned painfully, "If you want to pick fruit, go where there's fruit on the trees."

The place to begin is not among those who aren't giving at all or among the wealthy who are giving small amounts. The optimum place to start is among those who are already your top donors. Salespersons know this to be true in the secular world as well. The most likely person to buy your product tomorrow is the person who bought it yesterday. The same is true with charitable giving. The best donor prospect is the one who is already a committed donor.

But how can you get more from those who are already giving so much? Start with a personal contact. Invite the prospects to share with you their "likes" about the ministry of your congregation. This is not difficult. Top donors like the church a lot or they would not be top donors. Let them tell how the church — its strengths, its blessings, its joys — fits into their lives. Then ask how the prospect feels the local church could improve. Most top donors will have a response to this too. They may observe the need to expand the youth program or paint the sanctuary or replace the choir's robes. Then your final question may be, "And what are you, personally, willing to give or to do to make that happen?"

It is not unusual for highly motivated donors to give all or most of the funds necessary to accomplish these goals. "Well, how much would a youth worker cost?" one regular giver asked. When informed that a part-time person would probably cost $5,000 annually, the woman replied, "I'll increase my pledge $100 a month to get us started." A hundred-dollar monthly increase from only one donor! How many inactives would it take to generate this much new money?

STRATEGY 2. MAKE YOUR CASE

Why persons give will frequently determine *how much* they give. Can you give a compelling reason for increased giving in your local church? This rationale, called a "Case Statement" in capital campaigns, is just as necessary in a budget campaign. In order for persons to give more, they will need to see what more will *do*.

Thoughtful donors insist on what might be called a "contingent dimension" in giving. They want to be shown that, contingent upon the gift, something positive will occur. Conversely it must be

demonstrated that without the gift the desired outcome will *not* happen. If this causal relationship is not evident, many gifts will never be made.

Experiment with brochures, bulletin inserts, and newsletter articles that demonstrate what will happen if giving increases by specific dollar amounts. Try occasional closely targeted direct mail appeals to persons with particular interests. A solicitation to fifteen proven friends of youth may generate as much money for camp scholarships as a broadcast appeal to the entire membership.

STRATEGY 3. EXPAND THE INNER CIRCLE

At the core of most local churches (or most other organizations for that matter) is an inner circle of persons who make things happen. They make most of the decisions, do most of the work, and — not at all coincidentally — give most of the money. Congregations that are serious about upgrading the giving patterns of donors should consider expanding that inner circle.

Recruit persons with the ability to make a bigger financial contribution to the local church to become part of the core leadership. If more mission money is needed, get somebody with money involved in your mission committee. Access to inside information frequently increases awareness that increases financial support.

Psychologists point out that the best way to get someone to like you is not to do them a favor but to get them to do a favor for you. Ask persons on the edge of the inner circle to assume a significant job in the church. The commitment of the time required to teach a church school class may be all that is required to increase the financial commitment of that person as well.

6 THE GIVING PYRAMID

W here does the money come from in a typical local church? In spite of our egalitarian ideals and years of talk about "fair share giving," a small minority of persons basically finances the church (or any other institution for that matter!).

Unless your congregation is very unusual demographically or theologically, chances are pretty good that your income looks like the pyramid of giving on page 28.

The top 33 percent of the membership will usually provide 75 percent or more of the congregation's income. This disturbs people, and the leadership of the congregation will frequently complain about those who won't carry their weight. Occasionally the leadership will present campaigns based on what might be raised "if we all gave our fair share." They seldom succeed. Why? Because most congregations are not so homogeneous; it is not reasonable to expect similar levels of giving from a broad spectrum of donors.

Consider these reasons why persons give at different levels:

1. *Differing amounts of income:* That all persons do not have similar incomes should come as no shock to you. However, we must give some care to defining what we mean by income. For purposes of charitable giving, gross income figures are virtually irrelevant. What matters is discretionary income, money left after taxes and fixed expenses. These figures can be surprising.

The Center for Parish Development has published figures showing how discretionary income varies by age group. (See chart, page 28.)

Notice that because of the highest level of committed expenses — home mortgage, car, college, and so on — the mid-age members between thirty-five and fifty-five have only a fraction of the discretionary income of those older or younger even though gross income may be highest of all age groups. Perhaps more important, you have

THE GIVING PYRAMID

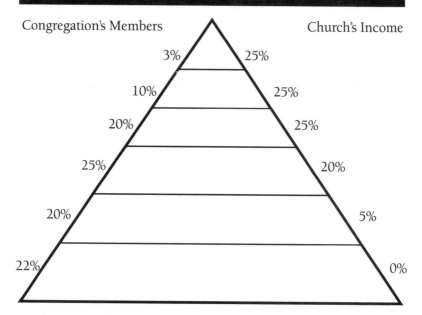

Congregation's Members

Church's Income

3%   25%
10%   25%
20%   25%
25%   20%
20%   5%
22%   0%

RELATIVE DISCRETIONARY INCOME

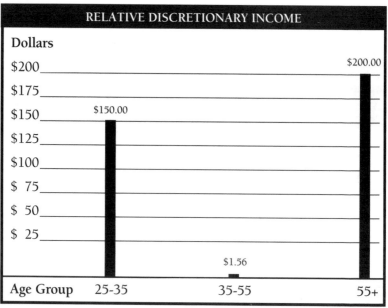

Dollars

$200 — $200.00

$175

$150 — $150.00

$125

$100

$ 75

$ 50

$ 25

$1.56

Age Group   25-35   35-55   55+

little or no control over this phenomenon. You may not agree with the priorities with which your members obligate themselves — $1,000-plus mortgage payments or $500 auto leases — but these expenses do exist, and every dollar of them is a dollar that will not be given to your local church.

2. *Differing levels of enthusiasm for the church:* To expect someone on the periphery of the congregation's life to be a core contributor is unreasonable. That is not how charitable giving gets expressed.

Secular charities have known for years that if you want persons to become significant donors to the organization, you must "plug them in" to the life of the organization. Give them a job, a leadership responsibility, or another opportunity for activity. Giving should jump at this point.

Many congregations find it difficult to appreciate the reality that evangelistic efforts are fund-raising efforts as well. Reactivating an inactive member may produce significantly more additional income than putting the "squeeze" on already active donors.

3. *Differing habits of giving:* Most persons base their current giving on what they have done in the past. That's good for those who are already giving at a high level but not so good for those stuck in the rut of lower amounts. Efforts to upgrade the giving habits of donors are not easy. Nevertheless, care must be taken to move folks along or they will be stuck at low levels of giving forever.

7 | POSITIONING: Establishing the Congregation to Receive

Twelve years ago Al Ries and Jack Trout published what is perhaps the single most significant marketing book in recent history. *Positioning: The Battle for Your Mind* (McGraw-Hill, 1981) describes the conceptual process through which marketers "position" a product in the mind of consumers.

Advertising executives Ries and Trout discovered that certain product concepts triggered predictable brand responses in almost everyone. To say "canned soup" to most folks meant Campbell's. Say "cola" and almost everybody thought of Coke or Pepsi. The trick to marketing any product is to create a place in the mind where that product is established. If you can't be the first or the biggest, perhaps you can be the cheapest or the best. In other words, find your place in the mind of the membership. This place, what advertisers call a "niche," is what will attract or repel contributions.

This concept suggests that contributions are attracted or repelled not by reality but by *perceptions* of reality. This is particularly significant in a church that is going through change. It is not what *is* that influences giving so much as how people *think* things are. Many older congregations may discover the perception that the church is failing. This feeling of failure is triggered not by any real failures but by the fact that the successes are not as great as during a previous period of success. Five hundred persons in worship is a large crowd today in most local churches. Nevertheless, the local church that once boasted 800 or 1,000 a Sunday may feel that 500 is a sign of failure. This congregation will experience a financial "double whammy." At precisely the time the congregation is most desperate for increased giving from the membership, giving frequently plunges as many persons act on the assumption that, like the Titanic, the church is sinking. It matters not that authentic ministry is still being performed. In the minds of the members is the nagging *perception* of a failing church.

In the short-term view, an occasional crisis may be good for fund-raising. Many persons respond well to a clearly articulated emergency need or even to a healthy sense of desperation. Notice the alarms sounded by such direct mail fund-raising. Oral Roberts was not the first to raise money with a figurative gun at his head. I once heard Richard Viguerre, the guru of modern conservative fund-raising, say that he could not raise money without something with which to scare people. Nothing brings in the checks as well as the occasional boogieman at the door.

But in the long run, successful fund-raising is just the opposite. It is next to impossible to sustain fund-raising in a negative environment. The local church that is always in the throes of economic crisis will soon experience diminished giving and economic decline.

WHAT MOTIVATES GIVING?

Some persons find it hard to grasp the idea that sharing a legitimate need does not always generate additional giving. It is "counter-intuitive." Let's pause for a moment and challenge this assumption about motivation. Is giving stimulated by *need* or is giving a *successful response* to need?

Take a look at where charitable dollars actually go. You will soon be struck by a dramatic phenomenon — Americans give the most, not to the neediest charities, but to the *most successful charities*. Americans love a winner. We want to be on the side of success. Father Flannigan's Boy's Town is one of the 100 largest charities in the United States today. Without being at all critical of Boy's Town, one should note that its endowment and other sources of income alone could sustain its work at a high level. Yet donors contribute millions of dollars every year to this famous charity. Why? Clearly not because of some catastrophic need, but rather precisely because that institution does its work so well. Gifts to Boy's Town produce a warm feeling within the donor who can fairly imagine Mickey Rooney himself sleeping warm under a blanket the donor's twenty dollars have just provided. The fact that no similar outcome actually was derived from this gift is quite beside the point. What matters is perception and a desire to buy into something successful and satisfying.

Do your donors experience such a feeling in their local church, or do they get the impression that the church is about to go out of business at any moment? If the latter impression is being experienced in your congregation, don't be surprised if giving begins to plummet. It is a rare (perhaps even a masochistic) donor who will continue to pour money into what appears to be a lost cause.

CHECK YOUR SIGNALS

Begin to examine the signals you are sending to your donors. Ask, "Is this likely to create the impression of successful ministry or of a sinking ship?" Donors who begin to doubt the effectiveness of their contributions often reduce the amount of their giving. Yet the financial leadership frequently responds with counterproductive messages about how the congregation *must* come up with the extra cash. In the name of truth-telling these leaders often send out a signal precisely opposite from that which might have stimulated extra giving.

As you evaluate the messages you are sending to the membership, consider the following checklist of questions:

1. *Is the message clear?*

One does not need to be a communications expert to recognize the gap that can exist between what the sender *meant* and what the receiver *understood.* Sometimes the confusion is caused by a lack of precision in wording. The notice in the congregational newsletter says, "First Church is running seriously behind in giving through last

"If everyone has their box handy I will proceed with the treasurer's report."

month." Does this mean that contributions are below previous years' levels for this time of year, that giving is behind projections for this year so far; or, as in many churches, that less than 8.3 percent of the budget was received last month? The first message is an indicator of a significant problem; the giving that lags behind expectations may or may not signal trouble; whereas the third possibility may be no more than a seasonal cash-flow phenomenon (especially in churches that receive 20 percent or more of their annual income during December).

If you mean to say that bills are going unpaid, perhaps that is what you ought to say rather than that "giving is running behind."

2. *Could we say the same thing in a more positive way?*

The statements "We're not giving enough" and "Giving is not yet at targeted levels" declare essentially the same reality. However, the first statement is accusatory and often triggers a negative, defensive response, whereas the second statement suggests a more hopeful situation.

When examining the profile of giving in a congregation, the finance committee may announce, "Some persons are not carrying their fair share." Not only is this unlikely to stimulate giving by under-performing members, but it may also tend to discourage the better givers. Consider, "We're grateful to those whose pace-setting giving helps us achieve our financial goals. Thank you for your leadership." Notice how the same message comes across with reinforcing power rather than as a "downer."

3. *Does the financial information presented suggest things are manageable or out of control?*

A caricature of Northern and Southern Europeans states that the two groups are diametrically opposite in the way they respond to conflict. Northerners may declare, "This situation is serious but not hopeless" while Southerners would say, "The situation is hopeless but not serious." In the church there is a fine line between creating a feeling that there is work to be done and suggesting that nothing can be done.

4. *Do the members of the congregation have adequate contextual information to understand the signals we're sending?*

Context clues are often lacking in the local church and often result in misunderstandings. For instance, how many times have you encountered the following situation? The Sunday bulletin contains an entry:

```
Needed Each Week..............$1,500
Received Last Week............. 1,387
Amount Short......................$  113
```

I must tell you that I have spent my professional life in church finance, yet I haven't a clue what the above entry *means*. Perhaps it means that a blizzard reduced attendance at last week's service. Maybe it means that recent home visits are beginning to pay off since even last week's Memorial Day weekend offering was nearly at budget levels. More likely, this message doesn't really mean anything of particular significance. In order to interpret the above data I need more information: What season of the year is it? What Sunday of the month is it? How much of our income traditionally comes in during the present month?

Perhaps your local church is an exception, but I have never encountered a congregation that received its income in fifty-two equal increments. More likely is the phenomenon of a four-Sunday month during which income is received something like this:

```
First Sunday......................$1,939
Second Sunday..................... 1,401
Third Sunday..................... 1,387
Fourth Sunday.....................  1,099
Monthly Total ..................$5,826
```

Even though 4/52 of the budget would total $6,000, this congregation is actually in good financial shape if this month is any month other than December when they commonly receive 15 percent or more of total giving. Why? Let's calculate a contextual expectancy of giving.

```
Annual Budget..............................$78,000
Typical December (15 percent of budget)....(11,700)
January - November Budget....................... 66,300
Weekly Need (January - November)............ 1,381.25
Weekly Average of Month Above ................  1,486
                              ($5,826 divided by 4)
```

This congregation is actually doing pretty well, but three out of every four Sundays it is reporting what appears to be failure. Few congregations can continue reporting this phenomenon without a negative fallout. Beyond the fact that such information is deceptive, manipulative, and bordering on dishonest, it may be counter-productive.

Finally, the trick in positioning is creating the image of success, even amid chronic economic chaos. This is not easy but can be accomplished when you understand what you're trying to do.

Celebrate even little victories. When your congregation completes a project, retires a debt, or initiates a new ministry, make certain that the whole congregation knows about it. Don't be afraid of bragging. The little success of which you brag may be precisely what motivates someone to see the local church in a new light.

Identify the image you wish to create about your local church, and reinforce that image in all your promotional materials. If you are "The Church That Cares," make certain that caring is evident in all you report. If your emphasis is missions, show the missional element in your every ministry. Don't try to be all things to people. Advertising experts like Ries and Trout point out that this is impossible. Create your position and use it to attract the gifts of the membership.

8 STATEMENTS: The "American Express" Plan for Increasing Income

W hen I received my American Express card bill the other day, I was reminded of one of the most powerful tools for increasing giving in the church — *statements*. These are an outstanding means of improving the giving level in nearly every congregation. In some local churches providing statements of giving will require nothing more than improving what already exists, while in other congregations virtually an entire new field is ripe for exploration. Whichever situation most nearly represents your own, sending statements is a strategy every church should examine. Here's how we can learn from American Express.

WHAT IS A STATEMENT?

For American Express, Visa, and Sears, the statement is primarily a bill. It's a way of communicating to the client how much is owed and how much should be paid at this time. I have seen some local church statements that also looked very much like a bill. Perhaps that's the look they were striving for, but I believe a statement of church giving should be much more than a billing. Although our statements are not entirely analogous with a credit card billing statement, we may learn much from the business world about this form of communication.

Even a cursory examination of a statement will reveal that the bill is merely part of a mailing package. Each component of the package has a special role in conveying, enhancing, and reinforcing the message to be delivered. Your local church giving statements can have an expanded life if you create a package of your own.

The basic components of our "American Express Package" are a minimum of five differing parts. Each part plays a particular role in delivering the total message to be conveyed. While successful packages vary in some of their contents, the five basic components include the following:

1. The carrier envelope
2. The promotional piece
3. The statement itself
4. A response device
5. A return envelope

Examine each component of the package with an eye to discovering the function each performs and how each function might be incorporated into your local church giving statements.

1. *The carrier envelope*

O.K., so there's really nothing surprising about the fact that American Express uses an envelope to send its package to us. It's basic, right? But it should be apparent that there is more to it than that. The first function of any carrier envelope is to get the package to the addressee and *on time*. This is the first checkpoint for us to compare our local church statements. Is your address file up to date? Do your members get their statements *on time?*

I have encountered dozens of churches where contribution statements lay in profusion on a table in the church narthex, sometimes weeks after they were prepared. These are statements that can make no "statement" to anyone, because they never get to anyone until it's too late. So lesson number one is, "Put a stamp on the carrier envelope and mail it immediately."

The second function of the carrier envelope is almost as important as getting the package to the addressee. This function is to get the envelope *opened*. If it is important enough for the giving statement to be prepared in the first place (and it is!), it's equally vital that people read it. They can't read it if they don't open the envelope.

Here American Express has a great advantage over us. Their addressees know that they *must* deal with the contents of the American Express envelope. In this situation a single, business-like carrier will do the job. Your envelope, on the other hand, does not require response by the addressee; that's merely what you hope for. Therefore you may wish *not* to make your statement look like a bill.

Take a quick reality check this week. Notice which parts of your mail you open first. Do you tear right into those window envelopes that are obviously bills? Is your first selection the big brown carrier that declares "You may already have won . . ."? Or are you like most folks and open first the mail that looks like correspondence from friends and relatives? What was the giveaway for you? Notice the characteristics of personal mail as opposed to a different category known as junk mail.

Personal mail is usually hand-addressed or at least has some personalization on the envelope. Could your local church statements be hand-addressed or customized in some way? Several congregations report good results through hand-addressed envelopes prepared by a volunteer group of older adults. Each month they address by hand the carrier envelopes for the entire mailing list. In some cases the volunteers also stuff the package. At any rate, whatever effort you make to get persons to open and read the giving contributions statement is worthwhile.

Some direct mail experts have strong feelings about the kind of envelope that should be used. Some say, "Use an unusual size or shape."

2. The promotional piece

In your promotional piece, tell what is coming up within the next few weeks. If it's September and new church school classes are being offered, say so. If it's December and you'd like to receive extra year-end gifts, include a piece promoting year-end giving. (Note: Excellent year-end giving material is available from the United Methodist Planned Giving Resource Center, P. O. Box 840, Nashville, TN 37202.) It's not enough to merely announce that something is about to happen. Tell why and when and, perhaps most important, how the event will make the church a better place.

Brag about your successes. People like to get good news. Make sure that some of what they get from you falls into that category. Tell about any success you've had. If more children and youth went to church camp this summer than in any of the past five years, say so. If the new hymnals are paid for ahead of schedule, share that, and thank the folks. Strive for a balance in the promotional material you include in your statements. Some news should be good, some should be challenging, and all should be truthful.

One special type of promotional material that should be a regular part of your package is an expression of thanks. At least once during the year, and ideally several times, include a thank you from someone who has benefited from the contributions of your donors. Persons who make great potential writers of these statements include the following:

- A child in the church school
- A youth home from camp or from a special service project
- A representative of a mission your local church supports
- A senior member who has benefited from the new ramp
- The church secretary who is pleased with the new office copier
- The pastor (preferably a personalized handwritten note)

Getting additional value from a package you're going to send anyway is good stewardship. Experiment with a variety of promotional and thank you pieces. Listen for and keep a record of comments. But most of all, look for increased results.

3. *The statement*

What do your financial giving statements say and what message do they deliver? Is this the same question asked in slightly differing ways? No indeed. A significant difference often exists between what something states and the message it delivers. With spoken language we accomplish this by using inflections in our speech. With written communication we accomplish this with well-chosen words.

The data on a typical local church giving statement usually include three or four sets of numbers. First is a record of the donor's giving to-date. This may be no more than a total or, with "one-write" forms in common use, may include the week-by-week giving record. Second is usually some statement of the donor's pledge-to-date. Third is the unnecessary recording of the difference between the pledge-to-date and the contributions. Sometimes this is denoted as "Balance" or "Balance Due." What was intended to be a friendly statement has suddenly become a bill. Finally, there may be provision for recording any extra non-pledged giving, such as special offerings.

How might this statement be improved? Probably the single most important change to improve the statement would be to recognize the difference between what we say and the message communicated. No matter what else is included in this mailing package, a phrase such as "Balance Due" makes the statement look like a bill.

Strive for a minimum of extra words or numbers. Because this is not a bill, why not attempt something more friendly? The basics of a local church giving statement should include the following:

- The goal (commitment-to-date)
- The results (contributions-to-date)
- Any special or extra giving
- Some expression of thanks

Each component of such a statement then conveys a message beyond the mere words. The four parts listed above will deliver positive messages. Here's how we read them.

- *Commitment-to-date message:* We promised we'd help you sustain this commitment, so here is the amount so far.
- *Contributions toward this commitment-to-date message:* We've noticed the gifts you've made so far; keep up the good work.
- *Extra giving message:* We noticed these too; you'll get credit for even the occasional spontaneous gift.
- *Thanks message:* We appreciate the confidence you place in us by making these gifts.

4. *A response device*

The point of any statement is to elicit a response. Your intention is to encourage additional giving from everyone who receives a statement. To do this, you, just like American Express, need a response device.

Perhaps the simplest example of a response device is a tear-off stub from the statement itself. The response should provide a place for the donor to indicate how much is enclosed. Remember that the church is a voluntary organization. Please don't take away the initiative of your donors. Let *them* determine how much the payment will be.

Consider providing opportunities for extra giving. If you have included a promotional piece on camp scholarships, encourage recipients to make a gift to the scholarship fund right now. Allow your response device to accept gifts toward a pledge, as well as any extra designations. I like to include a minimum of three lines on the response device — one for spontaneous gifts beyond the pledge, one for the current promotional target, and one for memorial gifts, mission contributions, and a variety of second-mile gifts.

You may wish to experiment with responses other than money. Encourage persons to share comments and other ideas with you. Perhaps all you need to do is include space on the response device with the heading "Comments." Some congregations have expanded upon this idea, encouraging this sort of communication with wording such as "An idea I'd like to share with the Finance Committee is . . .," "I'd like to hear more about . . .," or "I wish our church would . . ." Each effort to secure responses from the membership will allow persons to communicate their concerns in a manner other than withholding their funds.

5. *The return envelope*

Having examined statements from dozens of local churches, I remain convinced that the single biggest mistake common among them is not including a return envelope with the statement. American Express would *never* send a statement to a customer without including the vehicle with which payment could be made. Can you imagine MasterCard behaving like some churches routinely do? — "Here's your statement. Next time you drop by the bank, why not bring some money in?" Yet this is precisely the posture of many local churches. If statements are sent out at all (and many congregations send nothing), seldom does the local church include a return envelope.

Why is the return so important? Because you want *results*. You want to do everything you can to encourage the donor to write a check and mail it right away. Every impediment to this behavior will have the effect of diminishing returns.

If you want a particular response, make it easy for the prospect. Ask yourself how *you* react to billing statements that fail to include a return envelope. Do you pay them first, second, or last? My dentist recently changed his billing statement package to include a return envelope. Immediately, receivables picked up and turn-around time was dramatically improved. "I never realized how expensive it was *not* to have a return envelope," he told me. Now both of us are believers in return envelopes.

Here's a classic example of an area that can be checked out. If you don't believe a return envelope will make any difference, experiment. For a year, include a return envelope in statements for half your membership — say, last names beginning with A-M. Provide no returns for N-Z. Compare the results. How many persons mailed in money in their own envelopes? How much came in the return envelopes provided? Check your own results, and I am confident that you will do what dozens of other churches have done — place a return envelope in every statement.

Does the envelope require church-provided postage? Perhaps. You may wish to experiment with this as well. I would not recommend placing first class stamps on all those return envelopes, but

you might want to consider a business reply mail permit. This allows you to provide free return postage for your donors, yet you only pay for those envelopes that are returned. Currently the price for this service is a $50 permit fee plus an extra 40 cents above first class postage for each piece that comes back. The beauty of this strategy is that you are assisting donors to respond to your statements, but the only time you pay anything is when someone sends you money. Not a bad deal!

A FINAL WORD ABOUT STATEMENTS

Send them every month. American Express has never sent a quarterly statement to anyone. Visa thinks it's a false economy to attempt to save postage by mailing statements only twice a year. The "pros" all mail *monthly* statements and there is only one reason why. It works.

There are many reasons *why* monthly statements work. A fundamental reason is that monthly statements provide three times the opportunity for donors to respond compared to quarterly mailings. It's just mathematically superior.

Of more significance in the church today is the shift from seasonal to monthly economies for our members. For the vast majority of members under sixty years of age, the primary economic rule of their lives is monthly payments. Whether for mortgage, utility, or car payments, people today spend their funds monthly. When the church (or anybody else) tries to break this trend, they lose.

I have challenged dozens of churches to try monthly statements for a year. At the end of that time, if they were not convinced that the monthly frequency was worth continuing, I would pay all the increased postage charges. I haven't had a church collect from me yet. There must be something to it.

9 | THE STEP-UP CHART
A Three-in-One Winner

How do your donors decide how much to give to their local church? Perhaps more important, how can you influence them to give more? One proven strategy that pays off three different ways is the "Step-Up Chart" (see page 46). This simple gimmick is an adaptation of a traditional strategy.

For years stewardship leaders have known that sharing the giving profile of the congregation often increases giving. Herb Miller has taken this fact and has superimposed the giving profile upon these stairsteps. The result is a tool that has appeal on each of three levels: context, leadership targets, and general targets. Let's look at how and why the Step-Up Chart is so successful.

CONTEXT

The Step-Up Chart provides a *context*. It shows a donor where his or her giving fits into the total giving of the congregation. How else are persons to know how they compare? When I was a boy, the most common way for people to give at church was cash. We saw the gifts of others every Sunday as they passed before us in the offering plates. It wasn't difficult to see that most of the bills were fives, with a few tens and an occasional twenty.

Then we got sophisticated and began to use envelopes. Moreover, I now observe most folks placing the envelope into the offering plate *face down*. Today a look at the plates as they pass by will reveal little more than the backside of envelopes. What possible help can this be in informing my judgment about what others are giving? I suppose a case can be made that the giving of others is virtually irrelevant as a consideration for *my* giving. Nevertheless, for many persons it *does* make a difference.

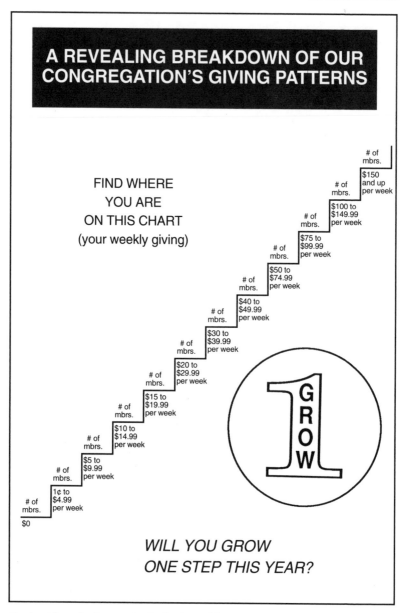

A REVEALING BREAKDOWN OF OUR CONGREGATION'S GIVING PATTERNS

FIND WHERE
YOU ARE
ON THIS CHART
(your weekly giving)

*WILL YOU GROW
ONE STEP THIS YEAR?*

The Step-Up Chart provides a graphic presentation of how the prospect's giving fits into the total giving of the church. After more than twenty years of unrelenting inflation, a chart such as this is useful to show us how our pledges compare with others. Funny, isn't it, how we learn to adjust other expenses for inflation but find a $20 bill still to be an impressive gift to our church.

Occasionally a participant at one of my seminars will look at the Step-Up Chart and wonder whether top givers will see how far ahead of the others they are and be motivated to take it easy for a while. Although this may be a rational concern, congregations do not report to me that this phenomenon actually occurs. Recognize that concepts such as "fair share" and "usual gift" are more properly the concern of under-performing givers than of leaders. A motivated donor is not moved much by the giving of others. A poorly motivated donor, however, may well find the giving level of peers to be instructive. Check this out next time you are solicited to contribute to a cause toward which you are lukewarm. You wish to contribute *something* but not a large gift. "What are others giving?" you inquire. Why? Because you don't want to give so little that you feel cheap or so much that you resent the gift. You will have discovered that, for some persons, the context really does matter.

LEADERSHIP TARGETS

The second thing the Step-Up Chart provides is a quick check-up for those who wish to be financial leaders. Nearly every local church has a number of folks who feel that they should be the top giver in the congregation, or at least among the top two or three. The Step-Up Chart gives instant feedback, showing these potential leaders whether they actually are leading the way.

Occasionally none of the persons who think they are the top donor really are. Sometimes the highest giving comes from a middle-class tither who is astonished to discover that he or she gives more than anyone else. I believe these persons deserve to know they are leaders.

Some persons may remark that this merely reinforces a childish desire to be first in line. I suppose this is true. However, we do not yet enjoy the luxury of a church filled with saints, and until we do, we must contend with some motives that are similarly imperfect.

I am not entirely convinced that a desire to be a financial leader is an unworthy motivation. It may indeed be a healthy expression of spiritual growth. When a person recognizes that he or she has the potential to be a lead donor and wishes to accept that leadership, this may be a healthy response indeed.

GENERAL TARGETS

In my judgment the most important function of the Step-Up Chart is its challenge — "Will you grow one step this year?" All Christians need an occasional challenge to improve their stewardship. Showing them the next step may be exactly what is needed for their growth.

"WE DON'T REFER TO A BOUNTIFUL COLLECTION AS HITTING THE JACKPOT."

Note on the chart that the intervals between steps are not the same. Toward the bottom the steps are no more apart than $5 per week. In the mid-range there is a $10 interval, and at the higher ranges, the top spread can be $25 per week or more. There's a reason for this disparity. The differential in increase is precisely how people grow. To challenge everyone to increase at the same pace, whether by percentage or by dollar amount, misses the point. Human growth — physical, spiritual, or financial — does not move relentlessly at the same rate. There are "slow starters," "catch-up artists," and "growth spurts" that occasionally surprise. Growth in giving is the same. I've never met a person who jumped from $2 per week to $20 and sustained it. Similarly, persons do not increase a $50 pledge to $52. The differing intervals of the Step-Up Chart recognize and reflect this reality.

Through the Step-Up Chart every donor will receive a target for giving that is appropriate for him or her to consider. The target will be challenging without being overwhelming.

10 THE ROLE OF THE CLERGY

C lergy are among my favorite people. My goal (and my pleasure!) has long been to assist the clergy in the task of leading the stewardship ministry of their congregations. Nevertheless, few clergy enter the ministry with more than a passing interest in the financial life of the congregations they serve. That soon changes. About the time their first parish refuses to provide a salary increase because "there's not enough money," even previously disinterested pastors develop an interest in improving their leadership in the financial ministry of the church.

Even when money is not a problem for the congregation, the pastor still has a significant role as stewardship leader. No matter what the current level of giving in a congregation, there is always room for improvement. The pastor's task, if nothing else, is to encourage and enable the church members to improve their stewardship.

CAN THIS ROLE BE AVOIDED?

Occasionally pastors will resist this challenging role. "Money is not my thing," they will protest. Or perhaps their views will be that financial planning is properly the responsibility of the laity (see Chapter 11). But, as with other fundamental pastoral tasks, pastors do not have the choice whether or not to be stewardship leaders. The pastor can only choose whether to be a *competent* or an *incompetent* stewardship leader. The reason a pastor cannot legitimately duck leading in stewardship is that all ministry has a stewardship component. Just as virtually every component of the church's ministry has implications for evangelism, so too is stewardship either encouraged or discouraged by virtually all we do.

MEANS OR END?

Is stewardship, particularly financial stewardship, the end or the goal of ministry? No, but it is close. Certainly a pastoral goal is to *build disciples*. Stewardship is such a fundamental part of discipleship that, it can be argued, authentic discipleship cannot exist without it.

Pastors perform the role of stewardship leaders as a *means* to any number of worthy ends — missions, outreach, youth ministries. Virtually anything with a price tag becomes an extension of the stewardship work that enables it all.

Stewardship in the life of most congregations, while a means, may be understood as a *quasi-end*. This enabling ministry is such an important means that it has a value of its own. Because stewardship is something a congregation does *now* while much of the results of stewardship will only be evident *later*, the means/end ambiguity is natural. For now let us simply observe that, means or end, stewardship must be part of the professional responsibility of each pastor.

FIVE STEWARDSHIP TASKS OF THE PASTOR

If the role of stewardship leader is appropriate for the pastor, *how* can this role be exercised? I believe that a good deal of this role will be determined by individual dimensions such as "style" and other personality characteristics. Although some clergy take to this role more naturally than others, I believe that *every* pastor can improve his or her skills by paying attention to the following five functional expressions of the task:

1. *Lead*

Leadership is a basic function of any leader. But what kind of leadership is appropriate? I have observed wide variations in leadership style among many effective local church pastors. Yet one critical role is a constant for all — the leader knows the way to the "promised land."

Historically, leaders frequently were literally out ahead of the followers. They blazed the trails and called to those behind to come along. Today I have been impressed by attractive models of effective leadership exhibited by some of my colleagues who lead in ways other than an "out-front" model. Evident to me now is, not the

"THE OFFERINGS MUST BE LOW AGAIN . . .
THERE GOES REV. RIPPLE WITH HIS GUM-
ON-A-STICK ROUTINE."

method of the leadership — out-front or behind-the-scenes — but that each successful leader must have a clear vision of where the congregation must be led to reach its goals (the "promised land").

This requires clergy to exhibit leadership that will catalyze the congregation rather than the other way around. In her final volume, the great anthropologist Margaret Mead reflected upon her career in anthropology. She noted that a common question presented to her was, "Is there anything unique about modern American culture from an anthropological perspective?" She went on to observe that a recent phenomenon was, apparently, absolutely unique among all the cultures she had studied. Dr. Mead noted that, in every culture, children and young persons learned from and copied the behavior of their elders, whereas in modern America just the opposite was occurring. In our society, so enamored of youth, adults have abdicated leadership in fashion and other cultural trends to the young.

In the church this phenomenon is very much in evidence as well. Young pastors are sent out to lead congregations, and some end up abdicating their leadership to the congregation itself. Pastors who are intended to be *leaders* become followers instead.

This role reversal would not be so bad if the pastors' first parishes were thriving congregations with strong stewardship programs. More commonly, however, the entry level situation for most young clergy is the marginal church with severe stewardship problems. These churches do an important service in the many ways they function to "rub off the pastor's rough edges," but in stewardship this is usually a different story.

Among the lessons taught to first-year pastors are a number of myths that hobble rather than enable future ministry: "Older members are on fixed incomes and should be left alone"; "I'll give, but pledging is not important"; "Our people are already giving all they can." Effective pastoral stewardship leadership will require the pastor to recognize myths when they are expressed and to help persons grow beyond these hobbling constraints of inadequate stewardship.

Growth begins with the vision of the pastor — a clear vision that he or she can articulate to the congregation. The pastor does not need to be the designated fund-raiser for the local church. (In fact, it is probably best if the pastor avoids fund-raising entirely.) Basically, the leadership role requires that the pastor be able to take the congregation to the next level of its stewardship journey.

2. *Teach*

A pastor was once pressed into emergency service as a substitute Sunday school teacher. With no opportunity to prepare a lesson or consult the curriculum material, the pastor attempted to stall for time. Looking at the seemingly hostile faces of these ten-year-olds, the pastor asked hesitantly, "Well, kids, uh . . . what shall we talk about?" Whereupon one lad replied with amazing insight, "Well, what do you know?"

That's the essence of the teaching challenge, isn't it? To teach implies knowledge, lore, something to be passed on. And where are today's clergy to acquire stewardship knowledge? From theological seminaries? Not very likely. Few are the theological schools that offer any stewardship education at all, and those who do frequently offer such a theoretical model that it has little relevance in the real parishes their graduates will serve. Sometimes these courses are taught by faculty members who themselves have never given pastoral leadership in the life of a congregation. Over the years I have had occasion to ask the presidents and deans of a number of seminaries why they offer so little in the field of practical church administration. All gave much the same reply. They did not offer such classes, they said, because the students were not interested in taking them. Incredible! There once was a time when schools called essential courses they deemed of value "required courses."

If the seminaries are not going to offer stewardship education, where can pastors acquire such training? While a variety of training opportunities exist, few draw much of a crowd. Perhaps the seminary leaders are correct when they say that nobody really *wants* stewardship education. Yet it is amazing to me how many other continuing education offerings have a wide audience, when few such events will have as profound an impact on the ministry of the pastor in his or her ability as a stewardship leader. Few pastoral careers are much influenced by their counseling techniques or their knowledge of Tillich. Yet hundreds of clergy are denied salary increases or adequate program funding every year because of inadequate abilities as stewardship leaders.

The acquiring of stewardship knowledge may begin with this book or other helpful volumes. Many good resources are available to give pastors solid grounding in preparing to *teach* Christian stewardship.

Teaching stewardship may take the form of an adult study unit on the theology of stewardship. It can also take a variety of more subtle expressions such as using stewardship language in describing the Sunday offering. A powerful message can be taught about giving when the pastoral leader looks for ways to teach stewardship.

3. *Preach*

Stewardship sermons ought to be among the best sermons preached, yet they often are among the worse. Stale, banal, canned sermons are cranked out every fall by pastors desperate to come up with something motivational to say. This use of the pulpit to create, at the last minute, a proper environment for commitment is seldom successful.

Sometimes stewardship sermons are ineffective because pastors know so little about the subject. Perhaps this is why so many clergy rush to the bookstores for somebody else's sermons on stewardship themes. I am no longer surprised by the enormous demands for my services in the fall of the year. I suppose I could preach in four churches every Sunday in October or November if I accepted every invitation. What about the preachers who are already in those parishes? Have they nothing to proclaim about their congregation's "giftedness" and the splendid opportunity to build a church-yet-to-be?

Frequently stewardship sermons don't work because they are inconsistent with the theology of the preacher. My friend Dr. Leo Waynick once analyzed the message of much stewardship preaching and concluded (rightly, I believe) that most of it is couched in the language of ethics. Giving is presented as a nice thing to do. In fact this was virtually the credo of Catholic faith for generations. Good people were givers. Don't give, and you're not good. Today The Roman Catholic Church has discovered stewardship, and giving is beginning to soar.

A pastor friend of mine is a fine preacher who can be eloquent and powerful about issues of importance to him. Yet every year he invariably "bombs" on two sermons in the fall. These are his attempts to preach stewardship messages. Apparently he has little conviction about this issue, and he appears to be desperately grasping for the words of others to fill the proclamation void. He tells old stories borrowed from others and presents a view of stewardship absolutely out of sync with the rest of his preaching.

A better alternative for most preachers is to avoid preaching a stewardship sermon altogether. Instead, learn to use stewardship illustrations in sermons all year long and create the context for commitment as stewardship themes underscore and reinforce your preaching throughout the year. Charles Allen's autobiographical work, *What I Have Lived By*, contains an insight into his preaching style. Whenever Dr. Allen discovered a powerful sermon illustration, he resolved to use it the next time he preached. It was better, he observed, to build one's preaching around powerful illustrative material than to attempt to adorn predetermined thematic material.

One can hardly read even the daily papers without finding regular helpings of stewardship themes and illustrations. Whether regarding environmental, financial, or governmental matters, stewardship material is readily available for the preacher who is prepared to use it.

4. Coach

The pastor as stewardship "coach" is not to be confused with the role as teacher. There is a profound distinction between one who teaches and one who coaches. While teaching involves telling about, helping to understand, and clarifying issues about stewardship, coaching takes these understandings to the next level, the level of practice.

The coach is the one who helps participants translate theory into reality. The clergy/coach creates an atmosphere where Christians may put into practice the concepts that the Leader-Teacher-Preacher has presented. For some participants this will require little more than to be invited into the game. Most persons, however, will need ongoing coaching to assist their growth as stewards.

The effective coach provides *motivation*. This will require more than "Win one for the Gipper!" exhortations from the pulpit. Effective motivation sustains the sense of enabling relationships between the act of giving and the ministries enabled. The coach knows when praise or prod is most appropriate and acts accordingly.

Sometimes the effective coach must demonstrate how a particular technique is to be executed. Just as a football coach might have to get down in a three-point stance and demonstrate blocking technique, the clergyperson must demonstrate through his or her own stewardship what a life of authentic discipleship looks like. Pastor, is your giving level consistent with what you preach about stewardship? Would your pledge be an inspiration to others? If not, your coaching ministry may require some improvement.

One of the most effective clergy/coaches I know performs this function in a masterful, yet entirely genuine way. Each fall this pastor invites to his home several persons whose growth in giving he has recognized. After dinner he challenges each one to match the pastor's level of giving. Because nearly all of these persons earn more than the pastor, they know that they should be able to match the pastor's pledge, and most accept this challenge. The pastor, a tither, then announces what his pledge for the coming year will be. It is rumored that a few faint dead away at this announcement and some may die on the spot. But most do go on to make substantial increases in their giving *as a direct result of the pastor's coaching!*

5. *Be pastoral*

If there is one role that has the potential of increasing the effectiveness of all the other roles, it is this one. *Be pastoral.* The pastoral dimension can go far in leading persons to new levels of discipleship. But what does it mean to be "pastoral"?

At the heart of this concept is the biblical understanding that the pastor *knows the flock.* This knowledge provides the personal dimension that helps the clergyperson decide who needs praise, challenge, or reinforcement. Yet I am discouraged in discovering that large numbers of pastors not only lack adequate knowledge of their parishioners, but purposely make little or no effort to know their members. "I don't *want* to know the giving of my people!" many clergy protest. "It might affect my preaching." Of course it will. It *ought to.*

I do not understand how a pastor can attempt to give pastoral leadership without any knowledge of the giving patterns of the people. Giving, after all, is a leading indicator of how one feels about something or somebody. Knowledge of the giving patterns of persons helps inform the pastor about a wide variety of issues relating to the spiritual vitality of the parish.

Most persons would have little regard for a physician who refused to know the blood pressures of his or her patients. Such a physician who preferred to treat all patients as if they had normal blood pressure levels would be guilty of nothing less than malpractice. Similarly, clergy commit a kind of malpractice when they act without adequate knowledge of the giving records of members.

THREE REASONS WHY THE PASTOR MUST KNOW ABOUT THE GIVING LEVELS OF PARISHIONERS

1. *Giving is a signal.*

It says something profound about the donor. Giving at a high level is a powerful affirmation that the donor appreciates and values the beneficiary. Similarly, low levels of giving suggest a lack of interest or commitment. To ignore these signals is to ignore significant parts of the persons themselves.

The pastor must recognize and respond to these signals in order to be able to offer pastoral assistance. The pastoral ministry is shrouded with enough ambiguity without a pastor attempting ministry unaware of significant factors that are readily available. If the church were no more than a fund-raising institution, this giving data would be important. But the church is much more than a fund-raising body. It is the Body of Christ. As such, the pastor's role then is to assist persons in their growth, service, and relationships within the Body. This requires nothing less than awareness of relevant information. Giving records are as relevant as anything else.

I once had the unfortunate experience of having my car's engine blow up. An oil leak had developed that should have been signaled by a warning light on the dash panel. Only after the disaster did we discover that the warning light was not connected. How many clergy, I wonder, experience the equivalent of a church "blow-up" absolutely without warning because they have "disconnected the warning light" on giving? The pastor needs to see the signals.

2. *Changes in giving are a call for pastoral intervention.*

What's the first thing persons do when they experience a mild level of displeasure with the church? Often the first response is to reduce the level of giving. This does not solve the problem, however. It merely announces that a problem may exist. But what happens when no one notices this reduction? The next step is usually a further reduction, followed by a complete lack of giving altogether. If nobody recognizes this action, the next step the donor takes will be out the door. Many persons of good will are unnecessarily lost to the church each year when a timely pastoral intervention might have redeemed the situation.

Changes in giving are not always triggered by dissatisfaction. They deserve a pastoral response nevertheless. For example, a member suddenly increases giving from $10 per week to $100 per week. On the surface this appears to be an affirmation of the church. A pastoral visit, however, may disclose a person recently diagnosed with cancer. This distressed soul is crying out for pastoral care, yet many clergy will not even be aware of the signs.

A colleague tells of a man who scheduled an appointment soon after her arrival as the newly appointed pastor in that parish. "Are you going to know the giving of the people?" he asked. Now that's a loaded question. Does the interrogator desire an affirmative or negative response? My colleague answered truthfully, "Yes, I will know the giving levels." To which the man exclaimed, "Good." Then he went on to tell how previous pastors had not wanted to know about their members' giving. He had recently experienced financial reversals culminating in bankruptcy and divorce. "The pastor never knew anything was wrong until it was too late," he shared. "Yet, if he (or she) had taken any notice of the precipitous drop in our giving, he (or she) would have known that something was obviously wrong." How many such cries for help are missed by clergy who don't want to know about money?

3. *Giving levels provide excellent criteria for selecting key leaders.*

No organization can afford the burden of uncommitted leadership. Yet local churches are routinely hamstrung by leaders who, though nice enough persons, have little commitment to the congregation. Positions involving decision making and financial administration absolutely require participation limited to those who have a stewardship orientation and *who are financially supporting* the church.

I regularly work with local churches in financial crisis. One of the most common contexts for those crises is a low level of giving among the financial leadership. Simply changing the members of the finance committee or the stewardship team from a pool of "those willing" to persons who are investing in the ministry of the church can make a dramatic change in the financial vitality of the congregation. Yet how is this possible if the pastor is unaware of the giving of the members?

SUMMARY

I have been making a case for the pastor to take an active role as stewardship leader. While different, individual styles provide for a wide variety of manifestations of these roles, I believe each individual role to be foundational to the task of discipling the church. Faithful pastors may experiment boldly to find ways their ministry can exhibit this leadership.

11 THE ROLE OF THE LAITY

J ust as there is a role for the clergy in stewardship leadership, the
laity also have significant tasks in creating a strong stewardship
environment. I regularly work with groups of lay leaders who are
actively engaged in the task of stewardship in the local church
regardless of whether or not the pastor is involved! This active
involvement is a blessing for the church and an important source of
stability for the congregation. Pastors, after all, come and go, while
the laity remain. The role of the laity, however, is significant enough
that it is crucial for lay leaders to know how to provide this stewardship ministry. Below I offer seven tasks appropriate for laypersons
involved in the stewardship ministry of the local church.

1. *Begin with your own stewardship.*

In the preceding chapter I observed how difficult it is for a pastor
to lead a congregation whose stewardship team consists of persons
who, themselves, have no appreciation of stewardship. As a committed layperson you will be making your greatest contribution to the
stewardship life of the church if you begin with yourself. *Make your
own commitment before you do anything else.*

Reflect on your giftedness. Ponder how God is at work in your life.
Then commit a portion of your financial resources to the building of
God's kingdom. Not only is this a spiritually healthy exercise, it will
prepare you to be used in mighty ways. Your personal stewardship
commitment will provide a foundation of integrity for your work as
a stewardship leader.

I remember visiting New York City years ago as a teenager. In
those days it was common for persons down on their luck to work as
walking billboards, trudging along the sidewalks wearing "sandwich
signs." I was struck, even as a youth, at the incongruity of the message and messenger. While the signs often extolled the delights of
some of the city's finest restaurants, they were worn by some of the

poorest, most underfed men in Manhattan. What could these men possibly know about fine dining? Their message had no credibility. As a lay leader in your congregation, does your current giving *underscore* or *undermine* your stewardship message?

2. *Commit to involvement in the finances of the church.* There is clearly a role for the clergy in the financial ministry of the church. (See the preceding chapter.) But this can never take the laity "off the hook." It is not enough to blame the pastor when money gets tight. Fault finding and blaming won't solve the problem anyway.

The financially healthy local church will have a pastor who accepts and successfully discharges the pastoral role. It will also, however, recognize that the responsibility for the ongoing financial program of the church belongs to the laity.

Pastors come and go. The laity provide the foundation for an ongoing financial ministry regardless of who's in the pulpit. When the local church allows the pastor to control the ministry of finance, three potentially negative outcomes loom:

a. The congregation becomes dependent upon the stewardship and finance skills of the current pastor — a risky proposition.

b. The funding campaign becomes a financial referendum on the popularity of the pastor. Even when such campaigns produce plenty of money, they do so for the wrong reasons. Loyalty to the pastor is a fine thing. It is not, however, an example of good stewardship.

c. The laity are cheated out of the opportunity to "own" their church's ministry.

Much has been written in recent years about the decline of involvement in today's church. The paucity of lay *men* in the church is particularly troubling. Yet the stewardship program of the church provides an excellent place for persons to work in a meaningful way. Whereas much of the church's program requires verbal or visual gifts, the stewardship ministry can be performed by any committed person of good will. In recent years the Rockefeller study (see above pages 9-10) documented strong correlations between volunteer activity and financial contributions. These data suggest that to deprive the laity of a strong role in the financial ministry of the church will result in reduced giving by those who might otherwise have been more actively involved.

3. *Recognize the difference between stewardship and secular fund-raising.* Laypersons often bring to the task of stewardship leadership valuable experience in fund-raising from secular arenas. Experience in United Way, alumni fund, and other community efforts provides a helpful context for work in the local church. It is *not*, however, the same thing.

There is an important distinction that must be noted between the tasks of stewardship and fund-raising. A healthy congregation will be involved in each of these at one time or another. Unhealthy churches frequently are found to practice fund-raising alone with no underlying stewardship base. The church is an environment different from that of a secular organization. Although the church exhibits all the characteristics of other entities, it is the arena for a uniquely Christian doctrine — Christian stewardship.

Stewardship is based upon an understanding of our giftedness. Its conceptual power lies in the universality of the claim that God has given us everything. Stewardship draws its legitimacy from this fundamental theological truth and, therefore, is not dependent upon case statements or dramatic local successes. It is a "motive for all seasons."

When times get financially tight, one is tempted to fall back upon familiar secular models based upon organization and promotion. This is fine and can enable you to share your gifts and experience with the church. Nevertheless, remember that stewardship is the one resource that belongs to the church alone. It is our blessing. It is that which provides financial "staying power." We ignore it at our peril.

4. *Create an environment where you can talk about money.* Observing the change that often occurs when laypersons move from their secular world into the world of the church is an interesting phenomenon. The same persons who occupationally speak freely and "let the chips fall where they may" often create, in the local church, a world of secrecy and financial taboos. "I don't want to talk about money in my church," a man once declared. "I get enough financial stuff at work." Let me ask a question, "Why do you suppose

money is talked about so often in a work environment?" Could it be because it is *important*? Perhaps the same truth would be appropriate in the local church. We must learn to speak freely about money because it is important, not in itself but because of the following:

- Money is a powerful indicator of our values.
- Money is a symbol many use for significance.
- The abundance or lack of money will influence everything else that is done in the local church.

We *must* talk about money in the church, and the laity are well suited to taking the lead in this crucial enterprise. Laity live in a world where money is recognized, valued, and seen in a context of legitimacy. Clergy, who live largely within the world of the church, frequently lose touch with the wider meaning of money. For some clergy, unhealthy attitudes may develop in which they see money as irrelevant, worldly, or even demonic. Living as they do on low levels of income, in borrowed houses, and with few opportunities for financial empire-building, it is not surprising that some clergy lose perspective about money. The role of the laity may be to provide a healthy check.

We *must* talk about money in the local church because its role in enabling or crippling the ministry of our church is evident. Even if we only accept the "necessary evil" premise about money, we must give it careful attention. Create an environment where you can talk about personal finances, goals, values, and how one's faith can touch each one. Encourage your pastor to become aware of the giving level of each member and actively to assist each one in stewardship growth. Such an environment may be the necessary step toward spiritual as well as economic vitality.

Finally, we *must* talk about money because Jesus did. Examine the teachings of Jesus. He spoke about money more than he did about sin. He spoke about stewardship more than he did about love. He spoke about money more than anything else. Fully one-sixth of all the verses in the synoptic gospels (Matthew, Mark, Luke) concern financial matters. Of the thirty-eight parables of Jesus, sixteen are about money and stewardship. The master talked about money because he knew the significance of it. Can we do less?

5. *Look for positive solutions.*

In spite of the occasional economic struggles we encounter in the local church, most situations can be improved. Taking a positive approach toward each situation may be all that is necessary to begin to turn around even the stickiest situation. A positive attitude is not mere Pollyannaism. It is rooted in two powerful phenomena that affect our work in the church. First is the fact that stewardship at the local level is intensely *attitudinal*. When we dramatize negative situations relating to the financial life of the church, we usually create the opposite result from what we desired. Bombarded with negative stimulae, donors tend to become paralyzed. Presented with positive opportunities, however, persons can and do grow. The second rationale for a positive approach is found in human nature. Persons like to be part of a successful organization. We love a winner. Presenting your local church in a successful context while offering specific positive opportunities for response will elicit more additional giving than any warnings about the catastrophes in store if giving doesn't improve.

Assist your pastor in presenting the challenge of stewardship as a positive matter with positive solutions. You will be doing far more than putting favorable "spin" on the situation. You will be creating a climate where giving can grow.

6. *Recruit other stewardship leaders.*

Laity have a splendid advantage when it comes to leadership recruitment. Because you are a leader yourself you have enormous credibility when you recruit another. Just as the best evangelism has been defined as "one beggar telling another where to find bread," stewardship is best when one practitioner invites another.

While I believe the pastor may appropriately assume a role in leadership recruitment, I nevertheless have observed that laypersons are often more successful in obtaining an affirmative response. Because the persons you recruit will be assisting *you*, you have a direct interest in getting competent people so you will have the best help.

Don't look for persons who are all like you. Recognize the wisdom of recruiting persons who complement your gifts and graces. If you are a detail-oriented person, look for creative thinkers. If you like to work behind the scenes, look for an out-in-front spokesperson. If you are young, consider an older partner or vice versa.

Far too many congregations have abandoned wonderful plans because of a leadership shortage. It is not realistic to expect the pastor to get all the necessary stewardship leadership. You are key to the success of this effort.

7. *Pray for the financial success of your church.*

Check out the most successful congregations in our nation, and one phenomenon is evident. Successful congregations are undergirded with a rich prayer life? Is yours?

Before the finance committee meeting begins, before the counters tabulate Sunday's offerings, before the campaign committee starts to contact donor prospects, pause to pray for the success of this holy work. Besides vague wishes for more money, have you actively prayed that God will help you find the resources necessary for ministry? Never underestimate the power of laypersons who pray for their church to be blessed.

When Charles Haddon Spurgeon, the great preacher of a previous generation, was at the height of his career as a preacher in London, he once observed that the reason many preachers had so much difficulty in proclamation was that "they are given 'ice-houses' to preach in." Prior to every hour of worship in Spurgeon's church was a prayer meeting of an hour or more dedicated to prayers for the success of the coming worship experience. Is it any wonder that souls were saved and lives touched during the next sixty minutes?

Perhaps you do not feel comfortable chairing a committee or speaking in a worship service to make financial announcements. Nevertheless, what's to stop you from quietly praying for the pastor or the other members of the congregation? Give careful consideration to ways God might be speaking to *you* about giving and service opportunities. You may notice a surprising power.

My prayer for you, lay friend, is that God might use you in a mighty way, and that through you the kingdom may become stronger. May God's richest blessing be yours.

Congratulations, Rev. Putnam. Your program to mobilize the laity
was so successful we don't even need you anymore!

Part 2

NEW
MONEY

12 | NEW MEMBERS — NEW MONEY

A somewhat obvious source of new money in the church is new members. Yet this potential pool of additional resource is frequently under-utilized. I regularly meet with local churches that have no plan at all for implementing the giving of new and prospective members into the ministry of their church. The hope is that new persons will voluntarily make contributions, but often little is done to facilitate this. It is not uncommon for new members to fail to receive even a set of offering envelopes, let alone a commitment card.

Even worse than this are certain disciples of church growth who refuse even to discuss giving with member prospects. I once met the pastor of a new congregation. This young man was complaining that the denomination was not providing adequate funding for this new local church start-up. After only fifteen months he had succeeded in building a congregation of nearly 200 members, but he was frustrated by a shortage of program funds. "What," I inquired, "are you doing to encourage giving from these new members?" Imagine my incredulity when the pastor informed me that they *never* talked about money in this new congregation. "We're trying to build a church, and we don't want to turn people off with financial demands," he declared. Turn people off? What kind of disciples was he creating here? Wouldn't a local church with an exciting program and the expectation of a high degree of discipleship be the most likely place to attract the kind of person with whom you could build a church?

Another pastor told me, "We're very careful not to come on too strong about money. After all, you can catch a lot more flies with honey than vinegar." I guess that's so if what you want is a bunch of sweet, stuck-up flies.

Ultimately you must decide whether you want numbers or disciples. This is a much more fundamental issue than the old quantity versus quality debate. It calls into question the relationship of new members and the ministry itself. Is your congregation to become yet another consumer-oriented organization that caters to the lowest common denominator, or are you to seek to call forth the best in people?

START WITH A VISION

Fundamental to this discussion is a vision of what the church is intended to be. If the church is primarily a program center where a variety of activities is available for a free-will contribution, then it is important not to alienate the customers. However, if your church is primarily a place for persons on a pilgrimage to discover and act out their personal discipleship, then we may — indeed *must* — challenge them to grow and give.

TRAIN THEM BEFORE THEY BECOME MEMBERS

One of the most difficult things to do in the church is to get persons to change. Much easier, however, is to help persons develop sound habits from the beginning. My friend and colleague Hilbert Berger summarizes the challenge this way, "Don't try to change the old, but thoroughly train the new."

Without much doubt the best time to elicit a positive financial response from persons in the local church is as they enter. As part of new member training and orientation include training in the following areas:

- The theology of stewardship
- What the Bible says about giving
- The program and ministry of the church
- The meaning of commitment

Establish the expectation that each new member will make a financial commitment *before* he or she is received into the membership. *This is non-negotiable.* Can you really afford to fill your membership with persons who will not make a financial commitment from the start? What is the likelihood that such persons will *ever* become committed if they won't commit now?

Many couples have learned that it is naive to live together outside of marriage with the expectation that "they'll commit later." Experience suggests that in such an environment they have little motivation to make a commitment and probably never will. Perhaps the problem of many persons in our local churches is that they too have settled for an uncommitted relationship with the membership and are merely biding time with folks who ought to be committed.

STRESS THAT DISCIPLESHIP IS ABOUT GROWTH

The amount of the initial pledge is not as important as it is that a pledge be made so long as new members recognize their need for growth. Younger members particularly are seldom able to make a major commitment such as tithing. Get them started with a pledge plus the expectation that their giving can and should grow over time. (See Chapter 9 on the Step-Up Chart.)

DON'T LOSE CONTACT

New members need to remain in a nurturing environment, thus many growing churches create church school classes from a new member class. A stewardship resource such as Norma Wimberly's book *Putting God First: The Tithe* would make appropriate curriculum material for a class of new members (see "For Further Reading," page 153). The pastor's contact also is very important. Expect the pastor to notice and respond to changes in the giving pattern of each member. Such practices will send powerful signals about the significance of commitment as well as offer needed assistance for the pilgrimage ahead.

Are there limitations upon our stewardship work with new members? Certainly. Among the biggest challenges is the values orientation these new persons bring with them to their new church. For instance, as consumers they are seldom much interested in making payments on pre-existing debts. The persons your new building helped attract will not likely arrive with a burning desire to pay the mortgage payments. Their openness to giving must be rooted in stewardship or in support for the program. Don't expect much loyalty or desire to pay a fair share. These attitudes may develop later, but, for the time being, new members primarily will be *reactive* in their giving. Give them plenty of reaction opportunities.

Of course, new members represent the future of the church, but there is no reason to believe that they cannot contribute meaningfully to the *current* ministry as well.

13 THE "PACK-A-PEW" METHOD

C heck with your local church's financial secretary and you will receive confirmation of an obvious, yet critical, trend — the relationship between worship attendance and giving. When attendance is up, so is the offering, and vice versa.

This suggests that virtually anything you can do to increase the size of Sunday's attendance will produce new money for your local church. Below are examples of proven methods of packing the pews in ways that produce additional income for your congregation.

- Invite the volunteer fire department to be recognized on a special Sunday. Give the department an award for Community Service or a similar recognition. Watch the pews fill up with new and contributing faces.

- Invite the high school choir or band to perform a selection or two. Along with the youth will come a variety of parents. This is a great evangelism opportunity as well.

- Ask members who are related to fraternal or benevolent groups to invite their colleagues to a reception they will host after the worship service on a specific Sunday. Many of these guests will come for worship as well.

- Include the children. In all my years of pastoral ministry, one phenomenon has been consistent: Whenever the children's choir or other children's groups participated in the worship service, attendance went up dramatically.

- Invite local personalities to speak. Ask the mayor, your congressional representative, local media personalities, or other "names" to give witness or greetings. Publish who's coming in your advertising, and you will begin to draw crowds.

- Give awards to community groups. Present a certificate to the local senior citizen organization or to another similar organization.

- Have a "Pack-a-Pew Sunday." The goal of this event is to fill the sanctuary. A proven strategy for this is to assign persons a specific number of seats to fill. The assigned person can bring relatives, neighbors, or friends to fill the seats for which he or she is responsible. Healthy competition can make this fun. If your church has a center aisle, for example, place someone in charge of each side. Have some type of award or challenge for the captain of the side with the highest attendance. One local church challenged the losing team captain to push the winning captain around the church parking lot in a wheelbarrow. Afterward a picnic was held, and the largest hunger offering in the congregation's history was received.

- Add another worship service. Here's a proven winner. Commit to a minimum of six months before you abandon this experiment, and odds are you'll never consider changing it. Ask yourself, "Who are we *not* reaching?" and design a service for them. The extra service(s) should not be a clone(s) of your regular service. As an alternative, how about a Saturday evening worship experience, worship at a nearby campground or resort, an early service, a communion service, or some other option? *Option* is the key.

  I once sat across the table from two pastors at lunch during a seminar I was conducting. These pastors, one a veteran and the other inexperienced, were talking shop. The older man mentioned that he had initiated a Saturday evening service aimed at single adults and was averaging forty persons each Saturday. The younger pastor reacted indignantly that he was not going to give up his Saturday nights for a handful of people. How many people does it take to make a worship experience worthwhile? And how many paying customers do we miss by refusing to offer additional options? Maybe this is one reason the older pastor was serving one of the largest churches in the area, while the young man was laboring in a smaller church.

- Highlight memorials. Have an annual Sunday when persons who have died during the past year are memorialized. Light a candle or place a flower on the altar for each one. Send a special invitation to the families of the deceased asking them to join the congregation for worship on Memorial Sunday when their loved ones will be honored. Include in the service a time to announce any memorial gifts. Make sure plenty of memorial gift envelopes are available in the pew racks. (It's amazing what will come in that day simply from the opportunity to make a memorial gift on Memorial Sunday.) Some local churches do this on All Saints' Day; others choose Memorial Day; but I prefer a Sunday in early January. This enables persons who died during the preceding calendar year to be memorialized. In addition, January provides a good post-holiday attendance booster.

The relationship between attendance at worship and giving to the church is well established. In fact, I substantiated this principle in *The Church Finance Idea Book* with what has come to be known as "Barrett's Law." This little aphorism observes the relationship between attendance and giving by declaring, "When they park it in the pew, they plop it in the plate."

14 USER FEES

One word best describes the attitude of many persons toward the ministries of the church today, and that word is *consumer*. Consumers have a limited desire to make contributions to support programs or causes for which they have little affinity. On the other hand, those persons frequently exhibit high levels of enthusiasm for *their* programs and projects. The concept of "user fees" is based upon this premise.

User fees are appropriate for several reasons. They share fairly the costs of specific ministries among those who utilize them. There is a certain equity or fairness to this arrangement. Similarly, fees allow the local church to recover costs associated with certain functions and services. Weddings, meetings, banquets, and other similar uses of church facilities have correspondent costs which user fees recover directly from the consumers.

User fees may also play a positive role as educational tools. Charging for costs associated with certain activities underscores the reality that these *are* costs. For the congregation to host an Alcoholics Anonymous group, sponsor a softball team, or offer child care costs something. A small charge for such services reminds everyone (including those who don't participate) that a cost is associated with this service.

Before you implement a user fee schedule, however, make certain that your congregation understands the rationale behind such a policy. Stress that requesting a fee is a way of placing the responsibility for specific programs upon only those who will use them. You may wish to experiment with scholarships or waivers in order to protect those unable to pay from exclusion. (Note: The prediction of the author is that you seldom will have an applicant for such scholarship funds.)

Begin by identifying the services you offer that are most likely to be used by the public. You may wish to make a distinction between non-members who are member prospects and those who clearly are not. For example, if a couple requesting a wedding in your sanctuary has been attending with some regularity, you may wish to waive the non-member fee as an expression of your interest in them. In most cases, however, non-members who want to be married in your sanctuary are pursuing this almost solely as a business proposition. You will be well advised to recognize this and to respond accordingly.

How much do you charge for the use of your facilities? Perhaps more important, how did you arrive at that figure? To charge $100 because "we've always charged $100" is to ignore the fact that your costs may have increased substantially. The absolute bedrock of user fees is to recover your costs. These costs will include utilities, custodial and other staff-related charges, plus wear and tear on your facilities. To these might be added a charge more representative of what other similar facilities charge. For example, what would it cost to rent an auditorium or country club for a wedding for 250 persons? You may be surprised to discover that the going rate could be $500 or more — and that's without a pipe organ!

Some well-intentioned members may object to fees of this magnitude on the grounds that they appear to turn the sanctuary into a profit center. Perhaps a better understanding is that this is no more than good stewardship of one of your most valuable assets. To use your building, which is a substantial investment, to generate a financial return is merely effective stewardship. *Not* to receive any return from this investment is questionable as a management practice. Another way of looking at this matter is that it gives non-members a periodic opportunity to support the church. If that means that a non-church-going family makes two $500 payments to your church in a lifetime, at least the weddings of their daughters were the occasions of some support for your church's ministry.

In addition to facility use fees, which look much like rentals, there is a wide variety of user-fee options. These include some of your most popular programs for members and non-members alike. For example, would persons be willing to pay a fee to participate in a church school class, a study group, or one of the church-sponsored sports teams? Many persons would find they hardly miss a $10 or $20 charge for these programs and may find that their commitment increases as they have invested in these ministries. (Check out Luke 12:34!)

Below is only a partial listing of services and programs for which user fees might be charged.

- Children's Choir
- Children's After-School Program
- Vacation Church School
- Youth Fellowship
- Youth Choir
- Handbell Choir

- Aerobics/Exercise Class
- Work Camp
- Bible Study Groups
- Pastoral Counseling
- Music Lessons
- Choir
- Child Care

Experiment with these and other possible user fees. Try to establish the principle that costs for all enrichment ministries will be shared (if not completely underwritten) by those who participate.

Certain fee-based programs may open up new ministry possibilities for your local church. A "parents' night out" childcare program might provide an attractive new service for your local church while potentially contributing new revenue for other ministries. Or how about older adult daycare? Not only would you be rendering an important community service, but you would be adding to your revenue potential.

In today's consumer-oriented world the church may need to re-evaluate its traditional stance of offering all services free of charge. I believe a case can be made that a charge for certain programs *enhances* rather than reduces their appeal. Our consumer-wise clients have learned the hard way that "free" seldom describes quality experiences. It is not exploitative to recognize this fact and to build fees into your church's ministry.

15 THE SECOND POCKET
Where the Real Money Is

A sk for a contribution, and the donor reflexively reaches into a pocket. Out of this pocket will come, depending upon the enthusiasm of the donor, a quarter, a dollar, or maybe a five. Studies document that 98 percent of these contributions come from some portion of the most recent paycheck received by the donor. It does not matter how the paycheck is received — weekly, monthly, semi-monthly — all persons tend to give out of their income. This is especially well-established for ongoing giving such as the weekly church pledge.

What happens, however, when we ask for funds for a new project or cause? Commonly the donor must decide among a limited array of choices:

1. Give out of the remaining income.
2. Reallocate giving among already established causes and the new appeal.
3. Refuse the new charitable opportunity altogether.

None of these responses is entirely satisfactory.

But what would happen if we changed the "pocket" from which the gift could be made? While the "income pocket" matches up well with many ministry needs — it's flexible, regularly replenished, and commonly contains untapped potential — income-giving alone is seldom adequate for dramatic increases.

The "capital pocket," on the other hand, contains an attractive array of potential gifts. This second pocket represents gifts from the *assets* rather than from immediate income and may be understood to be everything except income. The way I differentiate between the two pockets is to consider Pocket #1 to contain what persons *earn* while Pocket #2 contains what persons *own*. Either one may be the most appropriate source of the next charitable gift. Let's look at how this distinction gets realized.

THE INCOME POCKET

The income matches up well in the following situations:

1. *The younger donor.* When persons are just getting started in life, they seldom have had the opportunity to acquire much capital. Our lives and our giving revolve almost exclusively around the last paycheck.

2. *The ongoing ministry.* Some projects such as the local church budget are ongoing. They require an ongoing source of funding, and the income pocket fills the bill.

3. *The long-term pledge.* When we ask for a long-term commitment such as a building fund pledge to be paid over three years, we will likely receive a portion of the next three years' income.

THE CAPITAL POCKET

The capital/asset pocket matches up very well in a corresponding variety of situations:

1. *The older donor.* As our members reach or near retirement, their perceived ability to give more out of a fixed income becomes severely limited. (It does not matter whether or not this is actually true. It is sufficient that the donor *perceives* this limitation.)

2. *The "one-shot-deal."* Just as ongoing projects find their most appropriate support from donor income, specific one-time projects are most appropriately funded from donor assets. A capital project matches up perfectly with the capital of the donor.

3. *The major gift.* There are few persons indeed whose income is sufficient for making major gifts in the $10,000 and above range. These gifts usually must come from the capital of high income donors.

4. *Planned gifts.* Perhaps the best match comes when the donor considers a planned gift such as a charitable bequest or a charitable remainder trust. These gifts are gifts from the capital project.

ADVANTAGES OF SECOND POCKET GIVING

Congregations that encourage giving from both pockets commonly enjoy a substantial increase in total gift income, as well as a variety of other positive outcomes. Giving becomes uncapped as the potential for additional giving skyrockets. Once a donor reaches the age of fifty or so, the second pocket may be expected to contain a hundred times or more what the first pocket held. Imagine what this does to capital campaign possibilities. Persons who could not have been considered prospects for major gifts when income was required now become some of the most lively prospects. It is not uncommon for an older adult in her eighties to give one of the largest gifts to a building campaign, even though her income may be modest indeed. Where could such a gift come from? The *second pocket*, of course.

Another plus from encouraging second-pocket giving is that it enables older donors, such as widows, widowers, retirees, and others, to participate more enthusiastically in supporting the church's ministry. Veteran members are frequently loyal almost to a fault. Yet they become frustrated by the limitations of a fixed-income lifestyle. Show them a new possibility for giving, and the reaction will be enthusiastically received.

Willie Sutton, famed bank robber of years past, upon capture was asked "Why do you rob banks?" His reply was instructive for us all: "Because that's where they keep all the money!" Why encourage giving out of the second pocket? Because that too is where the money is.

TAPPING THE SECOND POCKET

By now I have made the case for soliciting gifts from the capital of our donors as well as from their income. But *how* can you institute this exercise. Try these proven strategies for expanding the pool of potential resources.

1. Tell the story of "two pockets." Go ahead and use my metaphor of pockets on a regular basis. You will be reinforcing the concept and similarly broadening the base from which gifts can be made.

2. Help persons learn to think about the second pocket. Do occasional exercises with the congregation that highlight the opportunities for giving out of capital. The "ABCs of Giving" can be a fun way to help donors get in touch with their ability to give. The "ABCs of Giving" is played by selecting a letter of the alphabet and encouraging members of the congregation to ask themselves a series of three questions:

- What do I own that begins with this letter?
- Do I really need this?
- Could I give it away?

Have some fun with this concept while challenging the members to think seriously about gifts from capital.

3. Have a year-end giving emphasis on non-cash gifts. Remind your members of the tax and other benefits of gifts of property, securities, and other non-cash items. (Write the United Methodist Planned Giving Resource Center, P. O. Box 840, Nashville, TN 37202, for information on year-end giving brochures and other materials.)

In today's church the second pocket may be the ideal source of additional giving. Learn to emphasize the *source* of the potential gift and you can often increase the *size* of the gift.

16 THE RULES OF DESIGNATED GIVING

A sk a hundred laypersons and the majority will tell you they like the opportunity to designate how their giving will be used. Ask a hundred pastors whether they think designated giving is a good idea, and the majority will tell you how dangerous it is to encourage, or even allow, "gift steering." Both the 1971 North American Inter-Church Stewardship Survey (*Punctured Preconceptions*, Friendship Press, 1972) and the Rockefeller Foundation study of 1985 confirmed this dichotomy of attitude regarding designated giving. While designated giving is clearly popular, the possibility exists for the giving to be reallocated from budgeted first-mile projects to non-budgeted second-mile projects. What can be done to encourage extra giving to designated opportunities without eroding the financial base of the church?

The *management* of designated giving is crucial if the goal is to secure an increase in total giving. Mere reallocation, while providing more money for *some* ministries, inevitably results in *less* money for other parts of your ministry. Yet a well managed program of promoting second-mile opportunities can increase total giving by 50 percent. A well managed program is one that follows the rules.

• *Rule 1.* Establish the ground rules before you do any promotion or solicitation. The financial program of your local church is fragile. It cannot be allowed to fragment into a thousand competing voices. The first rule is to agree that certain rules — call them management procedures — must be established regarding giving in the local church.

• *Rule 2.* Know the difference between "first-mile" and "second-mile" giving. Just as a journey cannot progress to the second mile without first completing the first mile, neither can a local church's giving program. The first-mile giving in your local church is that which enables its basic ministry and benevolences. This is the budget. Reasonable persons may disagree about what items belong in the budget. What you cannot allow, however, is for persons to ignore the budgeted ministry and direct all their giving to second-mile favorites such as the building fund or a favorite mission. Establish the principle that designated giving will be encouraged in the local church but only when the first-mile budget is being supported. This can be a powerful incentive for regular support of the budget. Donors know that their opportunity to give to their favored second-mile project will be directly related to the success of the first mile. My children never cared much for salads. Yet, knowing that dessert would not be offered unless they ate their salads, they could be counted on to finish every course with the expectation that their reward depended upon it. Offering and encouraging a variety of designated giving opportunities can be just as powerful a motivator.

• *Rule 3.* The leaders' responsibility is to call attention to every opportunity for giving. Do not try to protect the people from occasional giving opportunities. If a neighbor family's house is destroyed by fire on Saturday night, you have an obligation to take an offering on Sunday morning. Rule 3 commits the leadership to encourage and promote second-mile giving.

This rule also recognizes that leadership in this context may be much wider than the elected official leadership. Occasional special opportunities may be called to our attention by anyone who becomes aware of a special need such as the burned-out family, a devastating hurricane, or a shortage in the local food bank.

Once you have implemented Rule 3 you have effectively uncapped giving in the congregation. Each donor can relax, knowing that his or her pet project also will receive a fair hearing and an opportunity for support.

• *Rule 4.* It is O.K. to say no. One of the most crucial issues relating to special offerings is the environment in which they are received. When high pressure tactics and exaggerated guilt are used, persons seek to limit the number of allowable special appeals. And who can blame them? If I don't have the right to say "No, thank you" without a challenge to my loyalty, my only protection from an offering to which I don't wish to contribute is to prohibit the offering in the first place.

When a church leader observes, "We have too many special offerings in this church," what he/she *really* is saying is, "There are some offerings to which I don't care to contribute." Establish an environment in which a person can decline to contribute without eliminating the opportunity for giving by someone else.

Establish the expectation that second-mile opportunities are not expected to be supported by 100 percent of the congregation. That is one of the key distinctions between a first- and second-mile project. First-mile ministry is supported by everyone, while second-mile projects will be supported by a limited constituency.

• *Rule 5.* Coordinate the timing of the appeals. A fact of marketing life is that one cannot promote three things at once and expect to do a good job of promoting all three. Limit the number of requests presented to the congregation during any given period of time. This may mean that someone's pet project must wait a month before it can do its fund-raiser so as not to erode the success of someone else's. This is a price worth paying, however, because the same protection from competition will be provided equally.

Recognize that there are certain "prime time" days when a special offering for almost anything will produce a superior result due to the larger attendance. Christmas, Easter, and Mother's Day usually bring larger-than-normal crowds. The congregation may wish to reserve offerings on these special days for those projects that require the largest response. I know a local church that underwrites much of its second-mile missions program through special Christmas and Easter offerings. While the rest of the year includes any number of appeals, the biggest offerings are always received on Christmas and Easter.

• *Rule 6.* Provide the "tools" for giving. Please don't make it any harder than it already is for donors to make their gifts. Provide offering envelopes each time. If you are not routinely providing generic offering envelopes in the pew racks each Sunday, you are making a tactical error. With these "tools" in place, a giving opportunity can be spontaneous, yet get proper crediting because the donor may mark the envelope with its included purpose. "Fire Victims," "Hurricane," or "Camp Fund" can be noted easily on the envelope.

In addition to the envelope itself, the "tools" for giving include adequate interpretation materials. Bulletin inserts are, in my judgment, widely under-utilized. Recognize that the worship service is prime time for interpretation. Increasing the levels of awareness of prospective donors immediately prior to the offering is the equivalent of a "point of purchase" display in a retail store. It's your best opportunity to elicit a response.

• *Rule 7.* Enforce the rules. It is pointless to have rules unless they are obeyed. If you institute the understanding that it's O.K. to say no, don't allow strong-arm pressure tactics. This may require an occasional reminder to constituent groups about their solicitation tactics.

One local church successfully safeguarded the rules by establishing designated areas where solicitations or sales could be conducted. Other areas of the church were off limits. On any given Sunday you may have in your congregation a widow who, after the offering, has just enough money to go out for dinner with her friends. But what happens when a host of youth accost her, imploring, "Mrs. Johnson, won't you *please* buy a ticket to our chili supper to help us go to summer camp?" While she may love the young people, her digestion may not be able to accommodate chili. And even if she could, is it fair for her to have to make an instant decision — support the youth or go out to dinner? Establishing designated areas for such ticket sales allows those who do not wish to support that particular cause to simply avoid that area.

• *Rule 8.* Provide feedback. In many local churches, special giving is the financial equivalent of a "Black Hole." Once the money is raised, no one ever hears about the cause again. Donors wish to know the results of their giving. At the very minimum announce how much was received.

One of the greatest masters of this technique was Bishop Dwight Loder. No matter what the offering or its amount, Bishop Loder had a way of announcing the total in such a way that more money was elicited by the very announcement. "Our memorial service offering came within $53 of being an even $2,000," the bishop would announce. And, spontaneously, several persons would write checks for $53.

Can a program of managed designated-giving opportunities really increase total giving? Yes, it can. Perhaps more important, there can be a positive symbiotic relationship between first-mile and second-mile giving. The desire to support the second-mile projects provides incentive for strengthened first-mile giving as well. If you're looking for a new source of income, second-mile giving is it.

We are pleased to announce that in spite of our reduced budget,
we were still able to afford a church organist.

17 | ENDOWMENT FUNDS

L et me make a bold prediction right now: Churches that try to operate without a functioning endowment fund will struggle into the twenty-first century. Not only is this concept timely in its importance, but it is also enjoying much support from donors. And it is this message from our donor base that we ought to note carefully.

Across the church, donors are insisting on a permanent or endowed fund through which to build the everlasting church. Let's examine why and how endowments work in the local church.

THE CASE FOR ENDOWMENT

There are, of course, individual reasons that may motivate a donor to prefer making an endowed gift to making an unrestricted contribution. Among the most frequently articulated reasons, however, are these common rationales.

1. An unrestricted outright gift may impose a real burden upon the congregation. Few local churches are well equipped to handle large gifts without turmoil and dissension. It is often a difficult and divisive experience for a local church to receive a significant gift such as a bequest and then discover that the congregation is in conflict over use of the funds. I am becoming increasingly skeptical about the ability of a local church to make rational decisions about almost anything when substantial sums of money are "on the table." Rather than experience the pain and discord of such traumatic experiences, many congregations are learning to head off the controversy by implementing policies calling for endowment of all undesignated bequests and major gifts.

2. Bequests and similarly planned gifts frequently are the products of a lifetime's work and accumulation. It is inconsistent to encourage immediate expenditure of the fruits of a lifetime. Persons often tell

me, "I've worked all my life to be able to make this gift. I certainly don't want the church to blow it all at once."

3. Once funds are spent, they are gone. No matter how important the project or ministry, can we ever be certain that any use is the best possible stewardship of the funds? Time has a tendency to change our perspective, and we often look back and wish we could reconsider a particular action. The endowment option may reduce the pressure of making once-and-for-all decisions by providing a much more open-ended option. As James Russell Lowell wrote, "New occasions teach new duties" ("The Present Crisis" in *The Treasury of Religious Verse*). Could he have been anticipating the need for permanent funds?

4. Endowment may allow the church to have its cake and eat it too. Endowed funds produce income for current expenditure in ministry yet also allow for growth. Thus over a period of time, we are able to provide for the ministry of our choice while retaining the principal to fund future ministry. In essence, an endowed gift keeps on giving.

5. Endowment provides a helpful target for memorial funds. Is the best memorial a flower that will wilt in a week, a VCR that will be broken in a decade, or a permanent fund for ministry that, like the church, will be preserved to the end of time? Many persons prefer to make living memorials that endure and touch the lives of new generations.

6. Endowment is a wonderful stewardship opportunity for the local church. A well managed permanent fund can enjoy what Baron Von Rothschild called "the eighth wonder of the world" — compound interest. This powerful principle can enable institutions such as the church to gain from their very longevity. On the following page is a chart demonstrating how a well managed endowment fund* can successfully balance the need for current distributable income and still achieve long-term growth of principal.

---

*Assumptions: *a.* Fund is invested in a balanced portfolio, *b.* Portfolio earns 13.5 percent, *c.* Portfolio distributes 6.5 percent interest annually, *d.* Capital gains are retained.

	PRINCIPAL	INTEREST INCOME
Year 1	$100,000	$ 6,500
Year 2	107,000	6,955
Year 3	114,490	7,442
Year 4	122,504	7,963
Year 5	131,079	8,520
Year 6	140,255	9,116
Year 7	150,073	9,755
Year 8	160,578	10,438
Year 9	171,818	11,168
Year 10	183,845	11,950
	BALANCE after 10 years $196,714	TOTAL INTEREST over 10 years $89,807

ESTABLISHING ENDOWMENTS
FOR THE LOCAL CHURCH

Before you can expect much interest in the concept of endowments, your local church will need to establish clear policies regarding the receipt, administration, and distribution of endowment funds. (Helpful resource materials can be obtained from the United Methodist Planned Giving Resource Center, P.O. Box 840, Nashville, TN 37202.)

Spend a couple of months preparing your policy statement on endowment funds. Draft the document with an eye toward addressing the questions that are being asked in the minds of your donors. Among these questions are the following:

1. Who will handle gifts to the endowment? Is this a trustee function or should a separate endowment committee be responsible?

2. How do funds get deposited into the endowment? Does the donor need to designate the gift "for endowment" or will certain types of gifts automatically become endowed? Some congregations, for example, establish the principle that all undesignated bequests and memorial gifts are added to the endowment fund.

3. Who will be responsible for investing endowed funds? Few congregations have enough experience to invest an endowment fund in a professional manner. Even when investment professionals are members of the local church, it is seldom a good idea to perform the investment function "in house."

Volunteer professionals have several difficulties to overcome when they undertake to invest their church's funds. First, there is an obvious conflict of interest. Next is the danger of taking too much risk in an attempt to "show off" with impressive performance numbers, or, correspondingly, taking too little risk in an attempt to avoid embarrassing "corrections." Even when these obstacles are avoided, investment decisions often tend to dominate the time at trustee meetings. Can you really afford to spend the time of your volunteer church leaders haggling over certificates of deposit and mutual funds? Most congregations would be well served to obtain professional investment counsel from a money manager, a bank trust department, or your denomination's foundation.

4. What sorts of ministries will be eligible to receive payments from the endowment fund? It is probably as important to cite expenses that will *not* be eligible for endowment funding as it is to note what can be funded. Many persons may be fearful that the endowment's income may render the giving of the congregation superfluous unless you are able to assure them to the contrary. Many have heard the mythology of local churches that had too much money. Build into your policy the principle that *endowment income will not be used for basic operating expenses.* You may wish to exempt building-related expenses from this prohibition but beware of the potential for endowment income to get in the way of your ministry.

The fundamental issue an endowment policy is intended to address is this: Can persons know that gifts to their church's endowment fund will really be a good thing? Your policy must establish a strong case that the endowment will enhance, not undermine, the ministry of your local church. Give special attention to the "what if" types of questions that will surface. You will be positioning yourself to receive gifts.

THE THREE STEPS OF AN ENDOWMENT PROGRAM

Like the church itself, your endowment will go through certain cycles. It is important that you know where you are in regard to these stages. Although you are naturally anxious to begin receiving funds, you must take care to avoid sending a premature message. Indeed, one of the key features of an endowment is timeliness. Funds come in and go out in a sequence appropriate to both donor and congregation. Don't push it.

The first stage in a healthy endowment program may be called *positioning*. This refers to the matter described above of creating your policies for endowments. Until these are in place, you are not positioned to receive gifts. Donors like (some even require) certainty. In an atmosphere of uncertainty donors may hesitate, and often the gift will not be made at all. When a responsible job of positioning has been performed, however, donors no longer need to operate in an uncertain environment. Their fears have been dispelled, and the gift is likely to be made.

The second stage of an endowment program is *programming*. This involves a series of events, or programs, to highlight the endowment itself as well as the ways donors may contribute to it. See the *Big Money* section of this book for ideas to give your programming stage a lift. This stage will usually take two years or more.

The third stage in this process is *promoting* the endowment. This is the supreme test and the place where many congregations fail. Promoting the endowment is a never-ending story. The task will *never be done*. Accordingly, you should not even consider embarking on an endowment campaign unless you are committed to a strong follow-through.

Promotion of your endowment ministry can take any number of forms including the following:

1. Regularly update and distribute endowment brochures.

2. Communicate how the endowment is enhancing your current ministry. Make sure that each grant or expenditure from the endowment is well publicized. People really do want to know how their money is being spent or used.

3. Commit to at least two programs each year. These events should highlight ways members can make planned gifts to the endowment.

4. Refer to the endowment on your church's stationery. "Have you remembered Christ Church in your will?" at the bottom of your stationery reinforces the concept of giving to this eternal ministry.

5. Do your grant-making in public. Arrange to have symbolic checks given to representatives from recipient groups during a worship service. This gives great visibility to the flow of funds and places a human face on each beneficiary.

I know of congregations whose successful endowment programs have built permanent funds, the income from which exceeds 50 percent of the annual operating income contributions. Imagine what you church's ministry could become with a similar infusion of available funds.

18 MEMORIAL GIVING

The news hit me like a tidal wave of pain — a dear colleague had died. What should I do to respond to this painful situation? I knew that I needed to do *something*, but what form would that something take?

For me, and for many other thoughtful Christians, a memorial gift to a favorite ministry of my colleague seemed the best way for me to show my concern in some meaningful way. Memorial giving can be the source of substantial new money for the church that knows how to get it. Let's examine some of the basics of an effective memorial giving program.

Memorials are based on the joint motives of concern for the charity and concern for the person to be memorialized. Either motive can be sufficient for a gift to be made, but the best situation is when both motives are present. Keep this in mind as you develop your plans for promoting memorial gifts. It is usually not enough to appeal solely upon the project itself. Sure, the roof may need to be repaired, but is this really the best memorial for Aunt Lucy? Clearly there should be some compatibility among the project, the person memorialized, and the donor. I know of a situation in which a widower was eager to make a gift in memory of his wife. As it happened, the first major giving opportunity was to provide a public address system for the church. The man was pleased to make the gift as a memorial. Only when the P.A. system was in place did the man have second thoughts about the implications of memorializing his wife with a "loud speaker" system. Although the gift was made, the enthusiasm behind it was long gone.

BEWARE THE "BRASS WHATSIT" SYNDROME

One of the certified impediments to increased memorial giving is the tradition of the "brass whatsit." In many congregations a tradition prevails of purchasing a variety of candelabra or other brass paraphernalia as memorials, depending upon the amount of dollars in the particular fund. Over the years the church becomes cluttered with such "whatsits" and the level of memorial gifts is seldom raised. It should be evident that such items seldom fill pressing needs in the church. These purchases of various baubles tend to trivialize what could be a significant opportunity for giving. Commit yourself to expanding these horizons.

PROVIDE A VARIETY OF MEMORIAL GIVING TARGETS

One effective method to raise the level of giving to the memorial fund is to offer regular suggestions for memorial gifts. At the very minimum, your congregation should have at least two options for memorial contributions — an endowment and a current opportunity. Better still would be a variety of each option — a building improvement endowment, a missions endowment, a scholarship endowment, and a program endowment, as well as several current project needs.

Strive to have memorial options in a wide range of price suggestions at all times. When one such option is completed, replace it with another project with a similar cost. Think of this as the church's Wish List.

Regularly publish your Wish List as an invitation for memorial giving. Include "big ticket" items as well as smaller, more modest opportunities. Your list might look something like the one on the following page.

Note the range of prices for the projects on the list. Try not to be exclusive or to shut people out, but strive to upgrade the awareness level of the potential for living memorials. One pastor recently shared with me that in the first year of initiating a published Wish List, his church had never had a project with a price of less than $2,000 that had stayed on the list for more than three months.

WISH LIST

ENDOWED MEMORIAL OPPORTUNITIES
Memorial Scholarship Fund
($5,000 or more for individual scholarship funds)
Memorial Mission Endowment
Building Improvement Endowment
Program/Emerging Ministry Fund

CURRENT MEMORIAL OPPORTUNITIES
Memorial Chapel — $400,000 (estimate)
Piano — $3,400
Office Copier — $3,100
VCR & Television for Church School — $1,200
One Earthquake-Proof Third World House — $1,000
Sponsor for providing *Upper Room* Devotional Booklets to Shut-Ins
— $300
Paraments for Sanctuary — $600
Tuberculosis Vaccine for 100 Haitian Children – $50
Pew Bibles/Hymnals — $10 each

HAVE AN ANNUAL MEMORIAL SUNDAY

If one goal for memorials is to receive "new money," a great way to position your local church to receive new funds is to have a well promoted Memorial Sunday each year. During this special service, recognize all who have died in the preceding year. Have special candles, flowers, or other recognition devices to honor those who have entered the Church Triumphant.

Send special invitations to the families of those who have died. Enclose in the invitation a copy of your Wish List or any other memorial giving opportunity. Make certain you enclose a memorial giving envelope along with a return envelope. Not only will a high percentage of these persons be present in the worship service, but many will also make memorial gifts.

THE JOB IS NEVER FINISHED

In my congregation approximately 2 percent of the members die every year. The potential for memorial giving is high and growing but never complete. The task of managing memorial gifts is too important to blend in with other financial responsibilities. A separate memorial giving secretary is a must, and larger congregations should have a committee of three or more persons. You'll get results.

A final word about memorial giving results. Don't push. Because of the emotional element involved in such gifts, care must be taken not to come on too strong. Inform; don't "sell." Create the right environment and watch the gifts come in.

19 CAPITAL PROJECTS

One proven magnet for new money is an attractive capital project. It is often quite remarkable how a congregation with a tight budget suddenly discovers that much more money is out there when a popular capital project presents itself. Giving can increase by 30, 40, 50 percent or more. Let's take a look at several of the factors that enable this phenomenon.

WHAT IS A "CAPITAL" PROJECT?

The most common capital projects are buildings and building renovations, property acquisitions and development, plus the purchase, remodeling, or expansion of parsonages. Each of these projects is primarily a *real property* project. To this list I would add a variety of *personal property* acquisitions as well — an organ or other instrument, vans or buses, and finally, the initial funding of an endowment.

The commonality of these projects is that they are *enablers* of ministry — not the ministry itself. A good capital project must be based upon this understanding. More than a few capital campaigns have failed because those leading them did not understand that an organ, for example, is not an end in itself. A case must be made that the organ (or elevator, boiler, van, or other capital acquisition) will enable something positive. That is the product of an effective capital project.

WHAT MAKES A CAPITAL CAMPAIGN WORK?

Among the commonalities of successful capital fund projects are a variety of components that are present in any successful fundraising experience:

- Committed leadership
- Recognition of the validity of the project

- Clearly articulated benefits
- Broad and deep support

In addition, capital campaigns must consider other features. The funds raised must not be at the expense of current giving for operations, benevolences, or other ongoing ministries. Giving to the capital project must be presented in ways appropriate for each donor — young or old, rich or poor. The capital campaign should enhance the current program at the church.

Leadership for a capital project should include four types of persons:

    a. Those familiar with the project itself
        (building committee members, trustees, and the like)
    b. Those familiar with the finances of the church
    c. Those familiar with ways to get things done
    d. Those who know how to conduct the campaign

Campaigns that fail often do so because of significant leadership voids. In working with more than a hundred capital campaigns, I regularly observe building committees attempting to do all the fundraising themselves. This ignores a basic reality — the persons who make up the ideal team to conceive, plan, and develop a capital project are seldom the ideal persons to raise the funds.

Recognition of the project's validity is not the same as having a valid project. Many a worthy project goes unfunded because the constituency has not recognized the project's validity. Successful projects have what fund-raisers call a "case statement" — a formal document in which the merit of the project is articulated and demonstrated or a much more informal statement. Whatever form the statement takes, written or oral, it is still a necessity. Until the case is made, the money won't be raised.

Articulation of the project's benefits is often a matter of simple repetition. As the congregation hears the story over and over again, it begins to "sink in." Communication theory suggests that a message must have five exposures before persons can really assimilate it. One benchmark of this articulation process is the number of times and the variety of media through which the message is proclaimed. Use of more than one communication medium is strongly advised. Some persons read all their mail; others don't. Your most active members will hear announcements during worship; inactive members won't. Vary the approach, and reiterate the message to make your case. *Breadth* and *depth* of support is the natural outcome of the articulation of benefits. It is, however, not inevitable. I once was lodged in an inn on the banks of a river in Pennsylvania known as "a mile wide and a foot deep." Some capital campaigns similarly suffer from lack of depth in support. In the section on *Big Money* I address strategies to fund major gifts for your ministry. For now, remember these underlying norms:

1. Successful capital projects usually require a lead gift of approximately 10 percent of all you will receive. If you cannot find such a gift, your campaign will suffer.
2. Major gifts seldom come through the mail or from the regular offering plate. They are given directly.
3. Major gifts are more likely to come from persons of moderate income who believe in the project than from wealthy persons who don't care.

HOW CAN WE AVOID EROSION OF CURRENT GIVING?

One of the major dilemmas of ongoing capital projects is the potential for reallocation of current operating income to the capital project. It is "cheap grace" indeed for a donor to split the same $20 into $10 for operating and $10 for the building campaign. Care must be taken to avoid this syndrome. Try these strategies:

• Stress that the best source of gifts for a capital project is usually from the capital of the donor (see Chapter 15). When all giving is taken from the same paycheck, all gifts are competitors. However, when the building fund gift comes from the bank account or another capital asset and the general fund gift comes from the donor's income, the two don't get in each other's way.

• Give your operations budget adequate promotion and interpretation. A fact of life is that "the squeaky wheel always gets the grease." Even a casual examination of local churches with operational erosion will demonstrate what's wrong. Churches with new buildings, organs, and elevators, most surprisingly, often spend a good deal of time emphasizing the capital project. Even if little is said, donors are reminded of the benefits of the elevator every time they ride it. During a capital fund drive your general fund operating budget will require *more*, not less, emphasis.

• Work hard at securing commitments for general fund support from all new members. Persons attracted to your church by the new education wing or parking lot seldom arrive with a burning desire to pay on your mortgage. Their giving will be almost entirely for support of the program ministry. You will need to recognize this and act accordingly.

WHEN IS A CAPITAL PROJECT APPROPRIATE?

Not every congregation is ready to attempt a capital funds campaign. Similarly, not every project is appropriate. Try the following checklist to evaluate whether your church is ready to undertake a capital funds project.

A Campaign Readiness Checklist

Yes   No

_____ _____ 1. Will the proposed project improve our church?

_____ _____ 2. Will the congregation readily understand the project's benefits?

_____ _____ 3. Do we have committed leadership?

_____ _____ 4. Will the pastor be supportive?

_____ _____ 5. Will the congregation be comfortable with any debt associated with the project?

_____ _____ 6. Will the total indebtedness be less than three times last year's total church income?

_____ _____ 7. Are there major donor prospects who are likely to support the project?

_____ _____ 8. Can we avoid erosion of current budgeting support?

_____ _____ 9. Are we prepared to assume the new responsibilities for ministry inherent in this project?

_____ _____ 10. Do we sense God's leading us to undertake this?

Unless you can answer these questions affirmatively, your church is not ready for a capital fund program.

Part 3

BIG
MONEY

20 WILLS AND BEQUESTS

A ny discussion of "big money" must include careful attention to wills and bequests as sources. Charitable bequests continue to account for the majority of major gifts received by both churches and other charities. Moreover, bequest income is increasing at nearly double the rate of current other giving.

If you want to attract truly *big* money you will need to be attractive to donors making bequests. Let's take a look at how your church can receive more big money bequests.

THE GIFT EVERYONE CAN GIVE

One of the dramatic outcomes from bequests is the inevitable upgrading of donors' abilities to make gifts — and major gifts at that! Because bequests, by definition, are given only when the donor no longer needs the asset, even persons of modest means have the potential to become philanthropists. Indeed, the largest gift in the history of one local church I recently worked with was given by a woman from circumstances so humble that her house (which was also given to the church) brought only $18,000. Yet this woman's estate, though modest, was large enough to be a substantial gift. Imagine the income potential to your local church if persons begin to tithe their estates. How much would such a gift be in today's world? With the exception of certain high real estate markets, probatable estates of middle-class persons tend to be in the $150,000-$200,000 range. From such estates, $15,000-$20,000 could come to your local church each time you lose a member. Invested at 6 percent, this provides $20 per week perpetually.

Wills enable a level of giving that is not only substantial but also easy to give. Why? Because there is little pain in giving away what you can't keep anyway. Bishop Roy Nichols once put it this way,

"Stewardship is exchanging that which we cannot keep for that which we can never lose."

A scene from an old movie illustrates this easy gift phenomenon. In the film "Fun with Dick and Jane," a yuppie couple experience a series of economic reverses and are reduced to borrowing money from a finance company. After receiving $2,000 from the loan officer, Dick and Jane turn to leave. Suddenly, through the door bursts a hold-up man who orders, "Everybody on the floor!" Lying on the lobby floor with $2,000 cash in her hand, Jane suddenly decides that this would be an excellent time to repay their loan. Imagine her surprise when the loan officer refuses to take the money. Both persons had, correctly, recognized that the cheapest money is money you can't keep.

Perhaps one reason many pastors and other leaders in our local churches fail to see the potential of bequests is because they are in an earlier portion of their own life cycles, a period focusing on accumulation rather than on distribution. Only later in life does the inevitability of distribution begin to become clear. Our task as leaders is to assist that portion of our membership that is ready to prepare for this significant stewardship challenge.

WHO BENEFITS FROM A
BEQUEST PROGRAM IN THE CHURCH?

If a bequest program is so promising, why do local churches do such a poor job of emphasizing these planned gifts? Probably because the leadership fails to see the benefits to the whole congregation. Before you decide to begin or to refrain from a wills/bequest program, consider who would benefit:

• *Older Donors.* Among our most elderly members are persons whose current income is severely limited. Many of these persons are of the generation when pensions were the exception rather than the rule. Their standard of living has little in common with younger retirees with company pension plans and plenty of inflation protection. Still, many of these older members love the church and earnestly desire to supports its ministry. Including the church as a beneficiary of a will is often a liberating experience. "I feel good about the church again," one woman once said to me. She had been frustrated and had felt guilty about not being able to increase her pledge to her local church in recent years. Discovering this new opportunity to express her stewardship gave her a sense of grace. "I know I'll never be able to give the church as much as I'd like to," she said, "but now I know I have been faithful." Encouraging this giving option for your older members is more than soliciting money; it is rendering a real service.

- *Younger Families.* Our young families can seldom be expected to be major contributors. The economic demands of buying a home, raising a family, and saving for college make it difficult for many younger families to respond to appeals such as capital campaigns. Local churches with effective bequest programs commonly receive enough bequest income that the demands for building-related projects are funded without the need to ask young families to give beyond their capacity.

- *The Church Leadership.* One of the overlooked beneficiaries of a bequest program is the leadership of the congregation. Imagine how much easier it would be to plan the church's ministry with income expectancies that are unaffected by things such as the local economy, attendance patterns, and the quality of last week's sermon. To have a steady source of major gifts, particularly when the funds are endowed, can provide tremendous stability upon which the congregation can base its biggest dreams for ministry. The leadership then can give their attention to ministry rather than to fund-raising.

STEPS TO AN EFFECTIVE BEQUESTS PROGRAM

As with almost anything of significance, a strong program that encourages *and receives* charitable bequests doesn't occur overnight. There are steps to be taken and bases to be touched before the plan begins to produce gifts. Many congregations have been frustrated with a lack of success resulting from attempts to accelerate the process by skipping important steps along the way. Take care to include the following procedures in this sequence.

1. *Send out the right signals.* As strange as it may seem, some local churches appear to be sending out the message, "Don't give us your money when you die." Whether or not this is the message *intended*, this is evidently the message being received by the membership. I once asked a man who had served as a local church treasurer for thirty-five years if he could remember how many bequests his local church had received during his tenure. After a pause for thought, he replied, "We've only gotten two bequests, both from non-members." Imagine! For thirty-five years that local church had been sending out the steady signal, "Don't!" and everybody had gotten the message with the exception of two non-members who presumably didn't know better.

How does a local church send out such an unintended message? Among the ways the congregations learn that bequests are not welcomed and valued are the following (based upon actual experiences I have encountered):

- The congregation is deeply conflicted over possible use of a bequest that has been received. Watch what sometimes happens when a local church receives a gift it is unprepared to handle. Factions develop, sides are chosen, and "blood is on the floor" until the matter gets resolved. Is it any wonder that members observing this phenomenon conclude, "I guess I won't put my church through this again."

- The leadership threatens the congregations with extinction if certain financial goals are not achieved. "Unless we can increase our income by $8,000 by December 31 we might as well go out of business," the finance committee declares. Who wants to leave funds to an organization that could be gone by the time your gift is received?

- Memorial gifts and bequests received in the past have been trivialized through frivolous expenditures. Some pastors or other leaders are seduced into spending bequest income on what they perceive as the most pressing needs, not necessarily the most appropriate uses for such gifts. While there may be no more pressing need than a new lawnmower for the parsonage, it is by no means obvious that a donor would desire his or her once-in-a-lifetime gift to go for such a project. Donor prospects occasionally ask me for assurances that their bequests will not be spent on matters they consider inappropriate. "I didn't save this money all my life just to die and leave the church money for toilet paper!" a candid woman once remarked.

What should be apparent by now is that each of these inhibiting factors has a "flip side." If you can avoid these gaffes, you can also begin to send out the correct signal.

The message we wish to broadcast is a single one: "It's O.K. to include the church as a beneficiary in your will. In fact, we wish you would."

2. *Act on the basis of fact rather than rumors or myths.* For example, nearly everyone has heard about "the church that had too much money." Indeed, maybe that local church really exists somewhere. Whether the local church that got too rich is real or imaginary, many persons *believe* that it's true. Whether innocently or as an act of self-justification, some people won't leave the local church money because they feel it would not be in the church's best interest.

Provide a rebuttal. Establish how your local church has planned for even "mega gifts" and will use them to enhance, not inhibit, its ministry. A sound Endowment Fund policy may be all that is needed to defuse the argument that the church can have too much. Be able to tell what will happen with bequest income. Will it be endowed? Will it be spent immediately? On what sorts of things will it be spent? On what will it *not* be spent? For some donors it is just as important to tell what will *not* be done as what will be done with their contributions. This information is necessary both to enable that the bequest be made and to avoid awkward restrictions or "strings attached." I know of a local church that received a bequest that can only be used to repair fire damage from a fire that begins in the church kitchen! Why such restrictions? Probably because the donor didn't know any better. Lacking any direction from the church concerning appropriate uses of bequests, the donor came up with his own.

3. *Emphasize wills, not bequests.* No matter how much your local church may wish to receive charitable bequests, recognize that an absolutely necessary intermediate step for the donor is the execution of a valid will. In spite of the obvious relationship between wills (the planned giving tool) and bequests (the planned gift itself), many donors with a charitable interest never complete their giving plans because they lack the necessary documentation — the will itself.

Promotional efforts should emphasize the need for everyone to create a will with or without any bequest for the church. When more persons have wills, the church will receive more bequests. It's as simple as that. But the reverse is also true. Unless your members actually create valid wills, your encouragement to remember the church will produce nothing.

Encourage your members to do sound estate planning for their own reasons. Charities have long recognized that the institution providing estate planning assistance stands an excellent chance of being included in the will.

4. *Provide regular estate planning programs for members of the congregation.* Because the market for creating a will is a comparatively small segment of the congregation at any given time, make this programming an ongoing part of your church's ministry. Persons who have no interest whatsoever in information about wills today may very well be interested a year from now. Why this change? Something happens in their lives. Someone is born, dies, marries, or divorces. Any of these life experiences creates a profound shift in a person's interest in such planning.

Wills Clinics, Estate Planning Workshops, and other events focusing on estate planning topics provide the informational background for your promotional efforts. (See my book *The Church Finance Idea Book* for details on hosting Wills Clinics and other events.)

Target persons for participation in these educational events. If your local church has an existing senior citizen group, ask them to host an annual estate planning program. In addition to general promotional notices in the church newsletter and worship bulletins, send direct mail invitations to persons over age fifty (or some other arbitrary age threshold). We do not exclude younger persons; in fact we hope they will come. The targeting is simply a matter of cost-effectiveness. Younger persons are just not as likely to respond.

5. *Keep a quantity of wills brochures in the church office and in the pastor's study.* Don't underestimate the importance of giving timely assistance when persons demonstrate a readiness to do something. One pastor had coffee with a widower after the funeral of the man's wife. The man observed that he ought to have a will written and inquired if the pastor knew anything about how to do this. The pastor merely sent the man a brochure from the rack in the church office. The widower subsequently completed his estate planning by providing the largest gift ever received by that congregation, even though he was never a member of the church!

6. *Promote wills with bulletin inserts and other regular communication tools.* Your local church has a tremendous advantage over other charities in that you have regular access to your donors. Yet many local churches overlook the media that are theirs alone. The bulletin insert is a unique church communication tool that holds tremendous promise in promotion. On the following pages are examples of inserts I use in churches with whom I consult. Feel free to adapt these to your situation. (Supporting collateral brochures on wills and other planned giving topics are available from United Methodist Planned Giving Resource Center, P. O. Box 840, Nashville, TN 37202.)

Your wills program can be the door to a virtually unlimited source of major gifts. Prepare your congregation to receive them. Promote the concept of the stewardship of accumulations. Program with estate planning in mind, and your local church will receive big money bequests.

YOU HAVE WILL POWER!

A Christian's will can be the instrument through which families are protected, peace of mind is achieved, and miracles happen. The distribution of your estate can be a satisfying expression of your values, hopes, and faith, or it can be a terrifying ordeal. It all depends upon what you do now to prepare.

A charitable bequest through a Christian will is a most appropriate expression of stewardship. Giving through your will is an easy way to make a significant gift of assets that could not be given during one's lifetime. Gifts of property, heirlooms, or investments are often achieved through a bequest.

You may wish to consider these four styles of bequest giving through your will.

1. **A particular item of property.** A stated asset, such as one's farm, piano, or an issue of securities, is easily given through one's will.
2. **A gift of cash.** A specified sum of cash can be designated in your will even if your assets are in another form. The non-cash assets will be liquidated and the cash distributed.
3. **A percentage of your estate.** In inflationary times, designating a percentage of your estate for the church makes a lot of sense. Many persons give tithes of their estate to several causes.
4. **Remainder gifts.** You may wish to direct that the church receive what is left after other loved ones you provided for are taken care of.

There is no ideal way to create a will for everyone. The only thing that is certain is that your will will not be truly yours until you create it. Don't wait any longer. Exercise your Will Power today!

Name _____

Address _____

_____

Phone_____

☐ I have remembered my church in my will.

☐ Please send me more information about charitable bequests through my will.

☐ I would like to discuss this with my church's development officer.

United Methodist Foundation of the West Michigan Conference
11 Fuller SE • PO Box 6247 • (616) 459-4503 • Grand Rapids, MI 49506

"Laying a good foundation for the future." I Timothy 6:19

USE YOUR WILL POWER!

Estate planning is the top legal concern of American families. Yet more than half of United Methodists have not made a will and far fewer have done any serious estate planning.

Why? The biggest reason is procrastination. People simply put it off. There are other reasons. The association of estate planning with death ranks high. A fear that the cost will be too high or the distrust of attorneys are other reasons. Then there are those who believe their estate is too small.

All of these reasons may be important to persons, but they are hollow. They are just not valid. Estate planning is for the living. It is something that should not be left for the last few years of life. Estate planning and making a will won't cause you to die sooner, and it probably won't make you live longer. It will give you peace of mind.

If you don't have an estate plan
— The state has one for you. If you die without a valid will, your property will be divided according to a formula. This is not the way you would want it distributed.

If you do have an estate plan
— You can provide for the security of your family and also provide for the ministry of Christ through your church.

Estate planning is the responsibility of every Christian. Wise use of your accumulating resources is a trust from God.

Persons desiring estate planning need professional help and should seek the services of a competent attorney.

United Methodist Foundation of the West Michigan Conference
11 Fuller SE • PO Box 6247 • (616) 459-4503 • Grand Rapids, MI 49506

"Laying a good foundation for the future." I Timothy 6:19

WHY SHOULD I INCLUDE THE CHURCH IN MY WILL?

That's a pretty big question. It's really a question concerning the place of the church in one's life. Yet, as more and more of us are learning to practice estate planning, this is a crucial question for thoughtful Christians to consider. Consider these reasons for including the church in your will.

1. It's a matter of values. A will is a "testament" — a testimony concerning the persons and causes important to you. When we remember a particular ministry in our will, it is a powerful statement that this is something we believe in. Conversely, omitting the church from our estate plan suggests it really wasn't an important part of our lives.

2. It's a matter of timing. Many gifts just can't be given during our lifetime because we still require the gift asset for our own use. Giving through our will enables us to give to the church when we no longer have need of the gift. This often enables us to make a more substantial gift than we ever could during our lifetime.

3. It's a matter of faith. Because we believe that "the church is of God and will be preserved until the end of time," we believe that giving to the church through our will is a faithful way to provide for ongoing ministry long after we're gone. This is an outstanding way to provide endowments for future ministries through our church.

Still have questions? We'll be glad to help you find answers. Just complete and return the response form below.

Name _____

Address _____

_____

Phone_____

☐ I have remembered my church in my will.

☐ Please send me more information about charitable bequests through my will.

☐ I would like to discuss this with my church's development officer.

United Methodist Foundation of the West Michigan Conference
11 Fuller SE • PO Box 6247 • (616) 459-4503 • Grand Rapids, MI 49506

"Laying a good foundation for the future." I Timothy 6:19

21 MAJOR GIFTS

From time to time healthy local churches receive gifts large enough to qualify as major gifts. These gifts represent a significant affirmation on the part of the donor and require recognition that some giving simply does not fit the usual pattern. One of the exciting aspects of this phenomenon is that the donor is usually more excited about the gift than is the recipient. Another significant issue with major gifts is that, by their sheer size, they can have a tremendous impact on the life of the congregation.

What is a "major gift"? While there may be variations on this threshold according to the size of your local church and the wealth of your donors, for our purposes let's consider a major gift as any one-time contribution of $10,000 or more. A pledge of $200 per week is a gift of $10,000 over a year, but it is not considered a major gift because it is not a one-time contribution.

Major gifts are classic examples of second-pocket giving in that they are almost always gifts of capital rather than income. With this in mind, begin to strategize ways to prospect for major gifts.

COMPILING A PROSPECT PROFILE

Who do you look for when you are "prospecting" for major donors? *Capacity* is one of the key criteria for this selection. Does your prospect have the capacity or ability to make such a gift? If the answer is no, do not expect a big gift. Even if the answer is affirmative, this only establishes the *potential* for major giving. Recognize, however, that capacity for giving is directly related to timing. When do you want the gift? If you can wait, the number of major donor prospects increases dramatically. If you can include estate gifts in this consideration, nearly all members will have the *capacity* for a gift of $10,000 or more.

The capacity for major gifts merely establishes a "suspect." Suspects are able to give, but you do not yet know if they have enough motivation for giving to become "prospects."

Interest is a second key component of the profile. Unless the suspect has demonstrable interest in your church, no major gift will be made, no matter how wealthy the suspect may be. Indeed, one of the most common mistakes in soliciting significant gifts is the confusing of means with interest. Wealth, per se, is no particular indicator of a major prospect.

An old story illustrates this phenomenon. A congregation needed funds for a building campaign, so the pastor and the building committee chairperson went to visit a wealthy, though inactive, member of the congregation. They were ushered into the man's office, and while they waited, they marveled at the luxury of the decor. They fairly rubbed their hands together in anticipation of a big gift. Suddenly the millionaire burst into the office and began to speak.

"I know why you're here," he said. "You're here to ask me for money, and from the looks of things, you probably think I can afford to give you a bundle. But before you ask anything, there are some things about me you don't know.

"For instance, you probably don't know that my aged mother lives in a very expensive nursing home. Her medicine alone costs more than $500 a month.

"And you probably don't know that my brother is retarded and must be kept in an institution. He needs physical therapy and speech therapy, and must be watched twenty-four hours a day.

"And I don't suppose you know about my sister. She got the call to enter the mission field, and she works in South America at some clinic.

"Now, since I don't give any of them a penny, what makes you think I'll give anything to you?"

Wow! But this establishes perfectly our case that *means alone* will not produce a major gift. *Interest* must precede any significant gift. Look for those who have a demonstrable interest in your local church. These may include long-time supporters, those who have made significant pledges in the past, and those who have a known link with your church's ministry.

Look for *motivation*. What does it take to convince a suspect that he or she should make a major gift? It may be the obvious — a great project worthy of support. It may, however, be something a good deal less obvious. A memorial opportunity may be exactly the right motivation to turn a suspect into a prospect. The memorial nature of the potential gift provides one more motivation for giving. In fact, many major gifts are made primarily as a means to provide recognition for a loved one. Your local church may need to rethink any tradition that limits or inhibits such memorial opportunities.

In addition to *capacity*, *interest*, and *motivation* look for *involvement*. Better yet, try to get those persons with demonstrated capacity and interest to become involved. For example, if you want a wealthy person to give a major gift to a capital campaign, recruit the person to a significant leadership position in the campaign. The Rockefeller Foundation study, "The Charitable Behavior of Americans," demonstrated a clear linkage between involvement and giving. Our anecdotal experience confirms this phenomenon as well as its "flip side." Wealthy persons regularly tell me how disgusted they are by attempts to solicit large contributions from them for projects already planned. "If my money is good enough for them, why not my ideas and advice?" these persons ask. In fact, it's a pretty good question. The scourge of the every member visitation is the complaint, "You only come to see me when you want my money." The same gripe is shared by major donor prospects who are excluded from the planning phase of a project but nevertheless are expected to make major contributions.

MAJOR GIFTS NEED CULTIVATION

Just as plants do not begin to bear fruit the minute the seeds go into the ground, major gifts similarly require a period of cultivation and nurture. The gift will be made or not made as much on the basis of your relationship as on the individual merits of the prospect. Consider the following guidelines:

1. Establish the principle that the pastor and one key layperson will always have a relationship with this prospect. Many local churches miss out on major gifts because the pastor was the only one

who maintained a relationship, and when the pastor moved, the relationship was lost. For the same reason, the contact with the prospect should not be limited to any one layperson either.

2. Work at discovering any particular interests the prospect may have. Develop a special survey to be hand-delivered to the prospect. This is not a broadcast, mass-marketing tool, but rather a device to be used only for prospects with whom you have already established a relationship.

The survey ought to ask about activities in the local church in which the prospect has previously participated. It's not uncommon for a newly appointed pastor to have no knowledge that an elderly member until ten years ago had been the church organist for twenty years. This person might be the ideal prospect for a major gift for a new organ, but only when you recognize that potential.

The survey ought to ask about areas of ministry of particular interest to the prospect. It does not matter whether your local church currently engages in such a ministry or not. It is important to recognize that a person with a passion for handbell music may be the source of an entire set of handbells. Similarly, if youth ministry is mentioned, this becomes a person to be contacted when the congregation needs "seed money" to employ a youth pastor.

The survey ought to invite the prospect to describe particular areas of the church that might be improved. It is interesting to note how this discussion of areas for improvement often generates an immediate major gift, as the prospect begins to clarify the need and to recognize that he or she has the capacity to solve the problem. This is frequently much more successful than any solicitation because the donor prospects, in effect, talk themselves into the gift.

3. Keep a file on each prospect and work it regularly. "Working" the file requires maintaining a continuing contact with the prospect. If you left the prospect's home with a promise to explore the cost of a set of handbells, get back to her with the data. If she told you her primary interest was foreign missions, send her a brochure on a denominational mission study tour.

Some pastors object to this special attention given to major donor prospects. Recognize, however, that this care is given to assist these individuals with their unique stewardship ministry. Just as persons with illness are crying out for pastoral care, persons with major gift ability are in need of assistance.

4. Ask for the gift. It is surprising that many major gifts never are made for the simple reason that no one ever asks for them. Ultimately, when you have established a relationship, developed a profile, and kept in touch, you still may need to ask for the gift. Go ahead and ask. The primary solicitation must come from one of the two persons (clergy or lay) who have maintained the relationship with the prospect. When there is a need for additional information, take with you the appropriate person to provide it. The request for the gift, however, will always be made by the contact persons named in No. 1 above.

The potential that a regular program of major gift solicitation can enable is so great that it cannot be ignored. Begin now to develop and cultivate suspects into prospects and prospects into donors. Your local church will be stronger, and you will be rendering a real service to your major donors.

22 RETIREMENT PLANNING AND CHARITABLE GIVING

A s persons approach or enter retirement, they also enter a time for evaluation. Giving thought to goals, plans, and lifestyle issues is a fundamental part of preparing for retirement. This planning process and its attendant emphasis upon values is an ideal opportunity for many persons to perform their most significant philanthropy.

Charitable giving, as I have emphasized throughout this book, is primarily making a connection between assets and values. Clear parallels exist with the process of retirement planning. In preparation for a retirement lifestyle, persons must make decisions regarding the following:

a. Where they wish to live. Now that proximity to employment is no longer a major factor, persons are free to explore alternative residence locales for the remainder of their lives.
b. What activities will be the foundations of their new "free time." Will it be golf, painting, or volunteering that sets the agenda for each new day?
c. How investments and savings will be utilized. For many persons a profound value shift must occur during the early years of retirement. Their established value system of saving for retirement must be re-examined now that they *are* retired.
d. What provisions will be made for their estates. Retirement is a powerful rite of passage that signals the need to plan for security during life and appropriate distribution after death.

It should be obvious that the church has a vital role in assisting each of these life-passage decisions. Moreover, the local church that appropriately shows the connections between secular decisions and Christian faith will almost inevitably begin to receive significant gifts. Let's examine how.

THE PLANNING PROCESS

Planning, at its simplest, is primarily a matter of problem solving. Solutions to recognized problems will begin to appear as these problems are faced and explored. Assistance in this process is commonly welcomed by persons faced with such a challenge. It is a pity, however, that most persons in our local churches must rely on secular sources for such assistance. Unless your local church is made up entirely of young persons, a regular series of retirement planning classes should be a part of your ministry. Even if your classes tend to be forums for outside secular professionals to make presentations, such programs become qualitatively different when offered in the context of the church.

Helping your members identify and examine key life-cycle issues can be an expression of corporate pastoral care. Members begin to see how their faith and their church fit into the new lifestyle of retirement. If nothing else, performing these tasks as part of a church group tends to break down feelings of isolation commonly experienced by the recently retired. They begin to see that they are not alone — nor need they be.

IDENTIFYING VALUES (AND LIVING THEM OUT)

Robert Browning described the retirement years as "the last of life for which the first was made" (from "Rabbi Ben Ezra" in *The Norton Anthology of English Literature*). There is a certain awesomeness about deciding what to do with the remainder of one's life. More and more, however, as new retirees enter the process in better physical and financial condition, the options are virtually without limitation. Retirement that is meaningful and fulfilling must rest upon value-based decisions regarding at least these fundamentals:

- Family
- Time
- Finances
- Philanthropy

For many persons, the church can provide a welcome answer to the dilemmas presented by such value-clarification. The local church that is sensitive to the new realities of today's retirees will have identified a veritable "gold mine" of human and financial resources.

Time, for example, is a new resource for the just-retired. Persons who were reluctant to assume leadership in the local church during working years may be delighted to say Yes! now that schedules are less oppressive. Try to think of nontraditional ways these new retirees can serve.

Working with youth, serving as camp counselors, participating in workcamps, or serving as church school teachers can be a great link between generations. In my years of camp leadership I made it a practice to include retirees on every camp staff. I seldom found that older staff persons were limited by physical limitations nearly as much as younger staff members were hampered by emotional immaturity.

Remember the established link between volunteering and charitable giving. Increasing the volunteer possibilities for retirees will produce an inevitable growth in giving. If you observe older adults participating in travel experiences, encourage them to go on Mission Study Tours, to participate and volunteer in mission projects, or to take part in similar experiences. It took me a long time in my ministry to discover that the cost of a $2,000 trip to the Holy Land, while beyond my budget, was not a major impediment to some members of our older adult group. Retirees who experience the satisfaction of a workcamp or mission tour become potent ambassadors who tell the story with a refreshing sense of urgency.

When values are discovered, a major part of the development process is already complete. Once you know those causes or persons that are significant to your members, you have only to assist those persons to give financial expression to their previously identified values. In fact, even casual observation reveals that persons need little encouragement to give to those persons and causes truly important to them. Watch grandparents with their grandchildren. They fairly lavish gifts upon them and do so gladly.

One of the greatest opportunities for charitable giving occurs when a donor supports two favorite causes at the same time. For example, a common conflict among older adult members is the desire to provide for the college education of grandchildren while still providing for the church. For many persons these seem like mutually exclusive possibilities — money given to one will not be available to the other. However, an exciting tool exists that allows grandparents with charitable interests to assist the grandchildren, their local church, and themselves — all with the same gift.

A solution for many persons is the "Grandparent Gift," an educational unitrust. The features of such a gift (outlined below) are that the gift is placed in an irrevocable trust, and the income will be paid to the grandchildren for a stated period at a stated rate. Upon the completion of the grandchildren's education, the remainder in the trust is given to the church or other charity. This charitable gift results in two dramatic advantages to the donor: First, avoidance of capital gain taxes, and second, a charitable tax deduction for the remainder gift.

Here's an outline of how the "Grandparent Gift" might look:

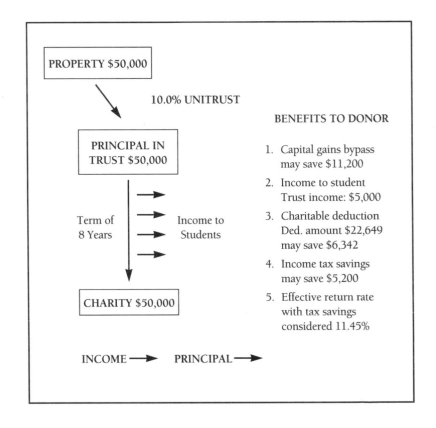

PROPERTY $50,000

10.0% UNITRUST

BENEFITS TO DONOR

PRINCIPAL IN
TRUST $50,000

1. Capital gains bypass
   may save $11,200

2. Income to student
   Trust income: $5,000

Term of   Income to
8 Years   Students

3. Charitable deduction
   Ded. amount $22,649
   may save $6,342

4. Income tax savings
   may save $5,200

CHARITY $50,000

5. Effective return rate
   with tax savings
   considered 11.45%

INCOME ➤   PRINCIPAL ➤

"You'll find *How to Live on Social Security* over there in the fiction section."

This is an example of a gift that is driven by donor motives and also solves two significant retirement planning problems for the donor — capital gains tax on appreciated property and income tax shelter produced by the charitable deduction. This strategy not only produces a larger gift than would be possible without the tax-free environment of the charitable trust, but likely results in a gift that would not even be possible after grandchildren are provided for through traditional giving.

Another significant retirement planning concern is the need for adequate retirement *income*. Investments accumulated during working years are often growth-oriented and produce little, if any, income.

Converting appreciated real estate into income-producing bonds has the negative impact of incurring a substantial capital gains tax. The tax bite on such a transaction is often 20 percent or more — a high price to pay for the privilege of retiring with adequate income. A solution to this common dilemma is a "life income gift" such as a remainder trust or a gift annuity.

Assets placed in such "life income gifts" may be sold without incurring *any* capital gains tax. This allows 100 percent of the value to produce income at predetermined rates. In the case of charitable remainder trusts, the donor selects the desired rate or amount of income. Gift annuity rates are established by the U. S. Department of Treasury and the Committee on Gift Annuities. (A list of current gift annuity rates can be found on page 141 of this book.)

Because there is an eventual gift in all "life income gifts" the donor qualifies for a charitable income tax deduction. This deduction, computed as the present value of the future remainder interest, may be as high as 50 percent of the initial funding or even more. Perhaps the best news about this deduction, however, is that it may be taken in the year the gift arrangement is completed even though the charity may not receive the gift for many years. (See Chapter 23 highlighting life income gifts for more detailed explanations of these strategies.)

Retirement is a significant rite of passage for those at that stage of the journey. In addition to being a time for the local church to provide supportive care for the persons at this crossroads, retirement can be the catalytic event for charitable giving. Help your members learn how their retirement years can become times of fulfilling service and satisfying major gifts.

23 | LIFE INCOME GIFTS

For your major gift prospects who are not multi-millionaires — and this means most of your members — a significant impediment to any major gift will be their own financial planning needs. The most common example of such a need is the requirement for adequate income in retirement. Even highly motivated persons who love the church are often reluctant to give an outright major gift because the gift assets are needed to produce income for retirement. For these persons the ideal major gift strategy may be a "life income gift."

Life income gifts vary in their complexity and applicability, but all have one common feature — the donor retains income either in a specified amount or at a specified rate for life. This ability to give and take — to make a gift while taking back life income — is usually critical in enabling the gift to be made at all. The good news, however, is that life-income-giving plans frequently offer such attractive advantages that major gifts are comparatively easy to market. Let's take a look at the most common types of life income gifts.

THE GIFT ANNUITY

Perhaps the oldest example of this gifting strategy, first developed in 1843 by the American Bible Society, is also the most popular. The gift annuity is a simple contract between the donor and the charity, obligating the charity to make payments to the income beneficiary — usually, but not always, the donor — for the remainder of the income beneficiary's life. (In the case of a couple, the payments are usually guaranteed as long as either income beneficiary is living.) In return, the charity receives a gift.

The charity or church usually invests the gift funds and uses the investment income to make annuity payments. When income from investments is insufficient to cover the annuity, the church may use the gift principal or other resources to complete the payment requirements. No matter where the funds come from, the income beneficiary must be paid.

Donors like the gift annuity for a variety of reasons:

1. Annuity income is assured and not subject to the ups and downs of investment performance.
2. The rate of the annuity, determined by the age of the income beneficiary, is often considerably higher than the donor can earn elsewhere. For example, an eighty-year-old can receive 9.6 percent from a gift annuity. Compared to other investment options this is quite attractive.
3. A portion of the annuity income may be received tax-free. Because this portion of the income is considered to be a return of principal, this portion will be free of tax until the principal-return is used up over the beneficiary's life expectancy.
4. The donor receives a charitable income tax deduction for a portion of the gift even if the church will not receive its portion of the gift for many years.

With these advantages readily available to our donors, it should be no surprise that gift annuities are among the most popular giving strategies. On the following page is a complete list of current gift annuity rates as established by the Department of Treasury and the Committee on Gift Annuities. For additional information, write to the Committee on Gift Annuities, 2401 Cedar Springs, Dallas, TX 75201-1427.

UNIFORM GIFT ANNUITY RATES

To determine the size of payments one person will receive from a gift annuity, multiply the rate shown on the next page for the person's age by the value of the property used to create the annuity. For example, a 70-year-old who creates a $10,000 gift will receive $780 each year.

Note: These rates are presented for informational purposes only. Before implementing any annuity gift, congregations should consult with their denominational office to inquire about any state or denominational regulations.

SINGLE LIFE

AGE	RATE	AGE	RATE
50	6.5%	70	7.8%
51	6.6	71	7.9
52	6.6	72	8.0
53	6.6	73	8.2
54	6.7	74	8.3
55	6.7	75	8.5
56	6.8	76	8.7
57	6.8	77	8.9
58	6.9	78	9.1
59	6.9	79	9.4
60	7.0	80	9.6
61	7.0	81	9.9
62	7.1	82	10.1
63	7.1	83	10.4
64	7.2	84	10.6
65	7.3	85	10.9
66	7.4	86	11.1
67	7.5	87	11.4
68	7.6	88	11.6
69	7.7	90-over	12.0

THE CHARITABLE REMAINDER ANNUITY TRUST

This life income gift arrangement has many similarities with the gift annuity but also has some significant differences. As the name suggests, this trust requires a formal agreement drafted by an attorney. The primary features of an annuity trust are the following:

1. Property is placed within the trust. This property can be cash but is usually appreciated property such as securities or real estate.

2. The donor retains the right to receive life income or to name another income beneficiary.
3. The trust pays a stated rate of income to the income beneficiary. This annuity never changes and is not influenced by investment performance, good or bad.
4. Trust assets may be sold without incurring any immediate capital gain tax liability. Thus 100 percent of trust assets may be used to produce the income stream for the beneficiaries.
5. Income paid to the income beneficiary is taxable but may offer certain advantages when capital gain property is used.
6. The donor receives a current charitable tax deduction for the "remainder" portion of the gift. This "remainder" is the amount expected to be left when the income beneficiary dies. As long as this remainder amount is 5 percent or more of the trust's initial funding, the trust may qualify for favorable tax treatment.
7. Upon the death of the final income beneficiary, the "remainder" in the trust is available to the charity subject to any restrictions established by the donor.
8. A final feature of the annuity trust is that, unlike gift annuities which are determined by donor age, the donor may select the *rate* of the annuity trust. As long as the required 5 percent remainder expectancy exists, the trust qualifies.

Because of the technical requirements necessary to qualify such a trust for the favorable tax consequences relative to charitable deductions and capital gain avoidance, only experienced legal counsel should be retained to create any charitable remainder trusts. (Prototype trust forms may be obtained from the Internal Revenue Service; ask for Revenue Procedures 89-21, 1989-1 C.B. 842 and Revenue Procedures 90-32, 1990-1 C.B. 546.)

A significant caveat for local churches considering assisting individuals in establishing annuity trusts is that a separate trustee should be designated. The local church should not serve as trustee of such gifts because of potential regulatory problems but also because of significant financial issues. Use your denominational foundation for a local trust department to serve as trustee of remainder trusts.

THE CHARITABLE REMAINDER UNITRUST

Like the annuity trust in its tax features, the unitrust is becoming more popular with donors because it can offer a significant additional advantage — inflation protection. While the annuity trust pays out a stated amount, the unitrust pays a stated *rate*. This feature allows for the income stream to grow as trust assets appreciate. For example, a $100,000 trust paying 7 percent will distribute $7,000 to the income beneficiary during the first year. If, however, the trust can earn 10 percent each year (not an impossible challenge) the trust will grow by the 3 percent differential between earnings and income distribution. As the chart below illustrates, the payout to the income beneficiary in the tenth year is more than $2,000 higher than the initial payment. For younger donors, such as recent retirees, the unitrust provides very attractive inflation protection. Over a life expectancy of twenty years or more, a 7 percent unitrust may return substantially more income than an 8 percent annuity trust because of the growing income stream.

HOW UNITRUST PAYMENTS MAY GROW OVER TIME

INITIAL TRUST FUNDING $100,000	RATE 7 percent
TRUST BALANCE	UNITRUST PAYMENT
Year 1 $103,000	$7,000
Year 2 106,090	7,210
Year 3 109,273	7,426
Year 4 112,551	7,649
Year 5 115,927	7,879
Year 6 119,405	8,115
Year 7 122,987	8,358
Year 8 126,677	8,609
Year 9 130,478	8,867
Year 10 134,393	9,133

Because the income payout can vary, the unitrust can receive additional contributions at a later time. This feature makes the unitrust an attractive retirement planning instrument, providing maximum tax shelter during working years and maximum income during retirement years.

Unitrusts, like all charitable remainder trusts, require competent legal counsel. Care must be taken in the establishment of the trust to provide for contingencies such as temporary inadequate trust income. Most unitrusts provide that the trustee may make additional payments ("Make-up") in subsequent years to compensate for a year when less than the scheduled payout was earned.

Prototype documents are available from IRS Revenue Procedure 89-20, 1989-1 C.B. 841 and 90-30, 1990-1 C.B. 534.

24 CHARITABLE USES OF LIFE INSURANCE

L ife insurance is the asset nearly everyone has. A person's life insurance may comprise half or more of the person's liquid assets in an estate. Life insurance is an asset that the donor acquired with the intention that it be given to somebody else. These and other reasons make life insurance a splendid tool for making major gifts. Insurance is not without its drawbacks, however, so let's examine how your local church can attract significant gifts of life insurance.

WHY LIFE INSURANCE IS A
SIGNIFICANT SOURCE OF MAJOR GIFTS

More than 85 percent of Americans own life insurance products. These products have the potential to produce an incredible distribution of funds — more than $2 trillion! Even if charities could receive only 1 percent of these proceeds, the total would be $2 billion for churches and charities across America. The potential here is simply huge.

Beyond the sheer size of this dollar pool, the life insurance product has properties which make it a remarkable candidate for use in providing gifts for the church. Among these properties are the following:

- **Flexibility** — Most beneficiary designations can be changed at any time.
- **Discretion** — Insurance proceeds often come to persons who do not require the funds for necessities. Portions of such proceeds can easily be given to the church painlessly.
- **Timing** — Insurance is a classic example of deferred giving, whether to personal or charitable beneficiaries. Action is taken today to accomplish a future result.

- **Objectivity** — Donors seldom identify closely with their insurance policies, unlike their feelings about their homes, savings accounts, and many other investments. Thus they are able to assign these objective resources beyond the immediate family where other assets are commonly distributed.

Life insurance offers donors an opportunity to make a substantial gift whether they currently have substantial resources or not. For example, a long-time church school teacher may wish to endow the church school's $3,000 annual curriculum expense. To provide this amount would require $50,000. While the donor may accomplish this purpose with a charitable bequest, this assumes both that the person will have $50,000 in his or her estate for gifting and that no current tax deduction is required. Giving by insurance may provide an opportunity to make a large gift at little cost and to receive current income tax advantages from the gift. Here's how it might work.

Donor Age (45) Female ....$50,000 Insurance

Annual Premium............................$ 1,059

Premium paid up after 7 years

Total Cost of Policy ....$ 7,413 ($1,059 x 7)

Income Tax Savings.......................$ 2,075 (28 percent bracket)

Net Cost of $50,000 Endowment ...$ 5,338

This example uses universal life insurance, an "interest sensitive" policy. Actual costs for similar policies may be higher or lower depending upon prevailing rates at the time of the policy origination.

Because the local church is owner and beneficiary of the policy, the organization may use the policy in a variety of ways long before the donor's death. The church may borrow against the policy's value. Although this will reduce the amount of insurance, the interest rate charged on such loans is usually substantially below bank mortgage rates. The local church may, in some cases, cash in the policy and use the cash for current projects. (Note: This should only be considered upon consultation with the donor and then only with donor approval.)

FOUR WAYS TO GET INSURANCE GIFTS

1. Ask for *obsolete policies*. As persons get older they may discover that the purposes for which they obtained life insurance originally are not longer valid. Such policies are obsolete in that their insured purpose no longer exists. Reallocation of such policies into charitable gifts is a fairly simple matter and can offer short-term incentives in the form of a current charitable deduction. Examples of such obsolete policies to look for include:

- *Policies to benefit children.* People commonly purchase additional coverage as their family grows. However, what are policy proceeds for, now that the children have reached adulthood? Many such policies could easily be contributed to the church simply by naming the church owner and beneficiary.

- *Education policies.* As in the case of policies for children, parents or grandparents often obtain insurance to provide for college education expenses in the event of death. When the children are through school, such policies can be cashed in or converted into charitable gifts.

- *Policies to insure a mortgage.* The phenomena of a new house, a big mortgage, and the purchase of additional insurance frequently go together. When the mortgage is paid off, what better way to celebrate and say "Thank you, Lord!" than to convert the policy to a gift?

The beauty of promoting gifts of obsolete policies is that they may be given with little pain or upfront cost. Unlike gifts of new policies, there is no further need for donor contributions, although many persons continue to make tax-deductible premium payments.

Gifts of existing policies also offer an extraordinary opportunity for capital fund raising. As long as the policy has current cash or surrender values, the church may cash in the policy and receive the best possible situation — a substantial gift and a living donor to provide future gifts. Donors frequently like to give these policies because they are perceived as "free" gifts. Insurance proceeds can be given without reducing bank accounts or other assets. Donors also get a kick out of watching such gifts go to work while they are alive.

2. Encourage life insurance gifts as *alternatives to bequests.* A sad-but-true fact of life is that some persons will never get around to creating a will or amending an existing will. In some cases this simply means no gift will be made. Persons who perceive the cost of an attorney's fees to be prohibitive are particularly hard to convince. Even these persons may be motivated to change the beneficiary designation of a life insurance policy. It's free and readily available — even to people with "lawyer phobia."

Changing the beneficiary designation on a policy is often perceived as less threatening than the creation of a legal document such as a will. Whether done with the retained right to change the beneficiary again, which offers no current tax implications, or done irrevocably with the attendant charitable tax deduction, gifts of existent policies are an attractive and simple means of charitable gifting without the need for an attorney's assistance or fee.

3. Encourage *new policies for endowment purposes.* As I have illustrated earlier in my example of the church school teacher's endowment policy gift, insurance often offers a means to maximize the amount of the gift while minimizing the cost to the donor. Particularly when the donor is comparatively young, the differences between cost to the donor and eventual benefit to the church can be striking. It is not common for the church to receive insurance proceeds of 5-10 times the after-tax cost to the donor.

If your congregation is looking for a way to give a new endowment program a dramatic boost, ask members of the committee to purchase life insurance gifts for the endowment fund. Imagine how much more viable the concept of endowment becomes when you are able to announce to the congregation that more than $500,000 has been pledged to the fund! This can often be accomplished with total first year premiums of $10,000 — $15,000 from committee members. This kind of leverage can change the attitude of a congregation concerning endowed funds.

Some denominations offer assistance to congregations that wish to implement insurance gifting programs. Such denominational assistance can provide valuable help in screening companies who lack the ratings or rates to make your campaign successful. Some denominational foundations provide additional assistance including the actual purchase of the policy to benefit the local church. Check with your denominational office to learn what assistance is available to you.

4. Ask donors to *tithe the policy*. With many policy proceeds in the $50,000-$100,000 range, even 10 percent of such a payoff can be big money. Moreover, your appeal will be using a familiar theme. Even non-tithers know about tithing, and many have felt the desire to practice it. This is an opportunity for them to do so at no current cost to them.

The Lutheran Brotherhood has pioneered the concept of including the church as a partial beneficiary of any policy. The results are astonishing, with millions of dollars subscribed through this means alone. Your church could benefit in this simple way.

I remember buying my first life insurance policy while I was still a university student. The policy was for $10,000 and the premium was $279. (How times have changed! Today I could buy twice as much insurance for the money even though I am twenty-five years older.) The agent simply inquired if I would be interested in including the university as a potential beneficiary. It was easy. I agreed to designate $500 of the policy proceeds for the university. At the time it was the largest gift I had ever made — and the easiest, too.

Experiment with other variations on this theme of tithing insurance proceeds. Some persons have gone beyond 10 percent and included the local church for a share equal to that going to their children. For example, if a donor has three children, he or she will split the insurance four ways and give the children and the church equal 25 percent shares.

Don't overlook the potential of other secondary beneficiary designations. In addition to being sole beneficiary or co-beneficiary, the local church could be named *secondary beneficiary*. Under this arrangement the church would receive the proceeds if the primary beneficiary has already died (or dies simultaneously). Your church may be named a *remainder beneficiary* which means your church will receive the proceeds only if the primary and secondary beneficiaries have died. This is not an uncommon phenomenon with single persons whose beneficiaries are often siblings. A final option that should not be overlooked is the *residual beneficiary* from annuitized policies or others with guaranteed values. If the insured dies before receiving the guaranteed minimum values, the residual is paid to the church.

IMPORTANT TAX CONSIDERATIONS FOR INSURANCE GIFTS

Because the incentive of a charitable deduction is often what it takes to complete a gift of life insurance, you will want to note carefully the tax implications of the following types of insurance gifts:

1. The donor names the local church the beneficiary of a whole life insurance policy but retains ownership of the policy. There is no current tax deduction but the proceeds are free of estate or income taxes.

2. The donor gives a paid-up policy to the local church and names the church the owner and beneficiary. The donor receives a current charitable deduction for the lesser of the cost or the replacement value.

3. The donor gives a policy to the local church. The policy names the church and donor's son to divide the insurance proceeds. The donor's tax deduction is reduced by 50 percent, the non-charitable share.

HOW INSURANCE CAN ENABLE OTHER MAJOR GIFTS

One powerful use of life insurance is as an enabler of major gifts. Sometimes insurance can solve problems created by other planned giving strategies. For example, when donors consider making major gifts to the local church, it is generally with the understanding that funds given to the church will no longer be available to children or other heirs. For middle-class donors this can be a serious impediment to major giving.

Insurance can often solve this conflict by providing an inexpensive method of replacing gifted assets so both the local church and the heirs can benefit. For outright gifts such as $100,000 gift of appreciated property, the current tax savings from the charitable deduction are often enough to purchase a single premium insurance policy that places another $100,000 in the donor's estate for heirs. In this case, in addition to the satisfaction of making a substantial gift, the donor also enjoys the tax-free conversion of capital gain property (which could be substantially reduced if sold with a tax liability) into a tax-free insurance proceeds for family members.

Wealthy persons can take an additional advantage from life insurance in conjunction with charitable giving. This strategy, called a Wealth Replacement Trust, restores gifted assets to heirs while also avoiding estate taxes. This trust requires competent counsel to establish. The trustee is given "Crummy Powers" (IRC 2503[c]), the right to make withdrawals of trust assets for the purpose of purchasing life insurance. Because the donor retains no "incidence of ownership," the insurance proceeds — commonly second-to-die insurance — pass to heirs outside the taxable estate.

When life insurance is used creatively, donors can often provide for heirs *and* charity at virtually no more cost than the traditional means of distribution to heirs. Here's an example:

Fair Market Value	Cost	Annual Income
$200,000 Rental Property	$50,000	$6,000

If the donor elects to increase annual income by converting this real estate investment to bonds, this sale of the property would trigger capital gains tax of more than $40,000. The remaining $157,000 ($200,000 FMV less $43,000 tax) could produce $10,990 annually at 7 percent.

If the donor's estate is subject to federal estate tax, the $157,000 bond portfolio would be further reduced at time of death by $53,380 of federal taxes at 34 percent. The heirs would receive $103,620. In this scenario the government gets nearly as much as the heirs do — $96,380 vs. $103,620.

A more tax-wise alternative would be to contribute the property to a charitable remainder trust. The property could be sold and converted into bonds without triggering any capital gains tax. Thus the entire $200,000 would be producing income. The same 7 percent would produce $14,000, $250 more per month for the rest of the donor's life!

The charitable deduction from the remainder trust could be $100,000 (depending upon the age of the donor), saving at least $28,000 in income taxes as well. The $28,000 in immediate tax savings plus the additional annual income from the remainder trust could fund the Wealth Replacement Trust. Depending upon prevailing insurance costs, the Wealth Replacement Trust should be able to purchase $150,000-$200,000 of insurance which would be available to heirs with no reduction from taxes. The charts below illustrate how this charitable estate planning, including the use of life insurance, benefits donor, heirs, and church.

EXHIBIT ONE: NO GIFT	
$200,000	Rental property
($ 43,000)	Capital Gains Tax
$157,000	Bond portfolio
($ 53,380)	Estate Tax
$103,620	to heirs
$ 96,380	to taxes
$ 0	to church

EXHIBIT TWO: CREATIVE GIFTING	
$200,000	Rental property
Convert to	Remainder Trust
$200,000	Trust
$150,000	Insurance (W.R.T.)
$150,000	to heirs
$ 0	to taxes
$200,000	to church

For Further Reading

The following titles are available from Discipleship Resources, P. O. Box 189, Nashville, TN 37202, (615) 340-7284.

Wayne C. Barrett, *The Church Finance Idea Book: Hundreds of Proven Ideas for Funding Your Ministry*. Order no. DR065.

Hilbert Berger, *Now, Concerning the Offering*. Order no. ST066.

Kenneth H. Carter, *The Pastor as Steward: Faithful Manager and Leader*. Order no. DR097.

Don Joiner, *Christians and Money*. Order no. DR096.

Don Joiner and Juanita Ivie, *Celebrate and Visit: An Every Member Visitation Program*. Order no. ST076.

Herbert Mather, *Becoming a Giving Church*. Order no. DR023.

Herbert Mather and Donald W. Joiner, *Celebrate Giving: A Financial Commitment Campaign*. Order no. ST073.

_____ , *Celebrate Together: A Financial Campaign Using Group Settings*. Order no. ST091.

Susan Patterson-Sumwalt, *Stories for Sharing: Exploring Stewardship with Children*. (children's resources for ages 3-11) Order no. ST099.

Norma Wimberly, *Dare to Be Stewards: Leader's Guide and Student's Manual*. (youth stewardship resource) Order nos. ST057 and ST056.

_____ , *Putting God First: The Tithe*. Order no. DR058.

OTHER RESOURCES MENTIONED IN THIS VOLUME

Charles Allen, *What Have I Lived By* (Fleming Revell Co., 1976).

Circuit Rider Commitment Program, available from Cokesbury, P. O. Box 801, Nashville, TN 37202. Order no. CC2-91 2210.

Al Ries and Jack Trout, *Positioning: The Battle for Your Mind* (McGraw-Hill, 1981).

Rockefeller Foundation, *The Charitable Behavior of Americans* (Washington, D.C.: Independent Sector, 1985).

ILLUSTRATIONS

1. By permission of Johnny Hart and Creators Syndicate, Inc., 5777 W. Century Blvd., Suite 700, Los Angeles, CA 90045.

2. By permission of Baker Book House, P. O. Box 6287, Grand Rapids, MI 49516. From *Instant Cartoons for Church Newsletters*, compiled by George W. Knight.

3. Reprinted from *Church Is Stranger Than Fiction* by Mary Chambers. © 1990 by Mary Chambers. Used by permission of InterVarsity Press, P. O. Box 1400, Downers Grove, IL 60515.

4. Reprinted by permission of *The Clergy Journal*, P. O. Box 162527, Austin, TX 78716.

5. By permission of Baker Book House (Knight, *Instant Cartoons*).

6. Ibid.

7. Ibid.

8. By permission of InterVarsity Press (Mary Chambers, *Church Is Stranger*).

9. Ibid.

10. By permission of Bo Brown, 218 Wyncote Road, P. O. Box 127, Jenkintown, PA 19046.

NOTES